Better Homes and Gardens®

YOUR KITCHEN

BETTER HOMES AND GARDENS® BOOKS

Editor: Gerald M. Knox
Art Director: Ernest Shelton
Managing Editor: David A. Kirchner

Associate Art Director (Managing): Randall Yontz
Associate Art Directors (Creative): Linda Ford, Neoma Alt West
Copy and Production Editors: Nancy Nowiszewski,
Lamont Olson, Mary Helen Schiltz, David A. Walsh
Assistant Art Directors: Harijs Priekulis, Tom Wegner
Graphic Designers: Mike Burns, Alisann Dixon, Mike Eagleton,
Lynda Haupert, Deb Miner, Lyne Neymeyer, Trish Church-
Podlasek, Stan Sams, D. Greg Thompson, Darla Whipple,
Paul Zimmerman

Editor in Chief: Neil Kuehnl
Group Editorial Services Director: Duane L. Gregg

General Manager: Fred Stines
Director of Publishing: Robert B. Nelson
Director of Retail Marketing: Jamie Martin
Director of Direct Marketing: Arthur Heydendael

All About Your House: Your Kitchen

Project Editor: James A. Hufnagel
Associate Editor: Walter D. Brownfield
Assistant Editor: Leonore A. Levy
Copy and Production Editor: David A. Kirchner
Building and Remodeling Editor: Joan McCloskey
Furnishings and Design Editor: Shirley Van Zante
Garden and Outdoor Living Editor: Beverly Garrett
Money Management and Features Editor: Margaret Daly

Art Director: Linda Ford
Graphic Designer: Deb Miner

Contributors: David Ashe, James Downing, Paul Krantz,
Jean LemMon, Jill Mead, Jerry Reedy, Marcia Spires,
Linda Strasburg

Special thanks to William N. Hopkins, Bill Hopkins, Jr.,
Babs Klein, and Don Wipperman for their valuable contributions
to this book.

INTRODUCTION

Imagine, for a moment, being invited on a very specially guided tour of your own house by the editors of Better Homes and Gardens®. The tour might begin in the kitchen, where we'd acquaint you with every aspect of this all-important room. Kitchen designers would help you analyze how well it works for your family. Decorators would advise how you could create a new look. Architects would show how to plan minor or major improvements on paper. Appliance specialists would inform you about your equipment options. Home management experts would explain how to hire and work with a contractor, how to finance major improvements, even how to best keep your kitchen clean, safe, and trouble-free.

Leaf through the pages of *Your Kitchen* and you'll find information, ideas, and guidance about all of these topics. *Your Kitchen* began when we perceived a need for a comprehensive, up-to-date book that would draw upon the experience Better Homes and Gardens® has gained in more than 60 years of serving homemakers. Our goal was to truly tell all about *your* kitchen.

Of course, the photos you'll see —more than 100 of them—don't necessarily show your kitchen as it is today, and you may even doubt whether it could ever look as good or function as well as the examples we've selected. Delve deeper into the book, though, and you may begin thinking differently about your kitchen. Maybe all it needs is a fresh styling motif, or a face-lifting of wall, counter, floor, and cabinet surfaces. Or perhaps you've been thinking about what a complete remodeling might be like. Photographs, floor plans, charts, and cutaway views help you explore all the alternatives—and tell how you can achieve them. We've even included three pages of templates you can use to get the kitchen of your dreams out of your dreams and onto paper.

Your Kitchen, more than three years in the making, is one book in a series we call ALL ABOUT YOUR HOUSE. This major, interdepartmental effort draws upon the talents and expertise of more than 30 Better Homes and Gardens® editors, designers, writers, and contributors, and explores every important element of a modern-day house. In other words, our tour of your home doesn't stop with your kitchen.

YOUR
KITCHEN

CONTENTS

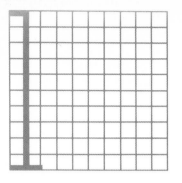

LET'S START WITH YOUR FAMILY

That's just where a good kitchen designer would start in planning your new kitchen. Because more than architecture, appliances, and even layout, your kitchen's success depends most on how it does what your family wants it to do. You don't need a drafting board—just a kitchen table where you can all gather round and talk. This overview chapter gets you started by asking the kind of questions a designer would ask—then the rest of the book shows what you can do with the answers.

WHAT'S YOUR FAMILY LIKE?

A look at your family tree—how large it is, how old it is, and how often it's uprooted—will tell you a lot about how you should plan your kitchen. For instance, a family with young, growing children clearly needs a different kind of kitchen than a couple whose kids will soon "fly the nest." That's why, to end up with a kitchen that's practically a member of the family, your family is where you should start.

Sizing up your family
A large family's kitchen needs more of just about everything (except maybe cooks). It needs more dining space, for sure, as well as more work space. But that's just the beginning; more meals to prepare also means more food and equipment to keep on hand and to store. And even if there's only one cook in a large family, that person needs ample space in which to work—which means a floor plan that routes all through traffic away from the kitchen. Chapter 4—"Getting a New Kitchen on Paper"—tells about planning traffic patterns for kitchens large and small.

Appliances, too, need careful consideration, since they'll receive more use by more users. A separate grill and cooktop may make sense. And when it's clean-up time, a large-capacity dishwasher, a disposer, and possibly a trash compactor can maximize efficiency. To learn about choosing the right appliances for your family's needs, see Chapter 5—"Selecting Kitchen Components."

The growth situation
Just don't get locked in to a design that can't "grow." The kitchen you plan today may not be the one you'll need five years from now. For example, you may be tempted to size shelving for the jars of baby food you're buying a lot of now, but what about ten or 15 years from now when those babies are teenagers? On the other hand, if your kids are already teenagers, you should probably be looking to the day when your kitchen will serve just the two of you. One- and two-person kitchens need more storage space for small appliances and convenience foods; less, perhaps, for large quantities of staples.

Your move
If your family doesn't stay in one place too long, your kitchen planning takes on yet another dimension—resale value. The kitchen of a "temporary home" is no place in which to be a compulsive remodeler. Instead, stick with a standard plan that incorporates efficient work centers, versatile storage, an eating area, and up-to-date appliances. Limit your customizing to small, easy-to-change elements, such as wall coverings or window treatments. Keep the basic surfaces—your floors, cabinets, and counter tops—neutral, natural, and generally appealing to most buyers. Chapter 2—"What's Your Style?"—shows you a number of possibilities in eight popular kitchen styles.

In general, try to anticipate the return on investment you'll net from every improvement you make. Should you build in top-of-the-line appliances, or mid-priced models? Or should you buy freestanding portables you can take with you? Don't just consider the money you spend, but also your time and hard work, and of course the inevitable inconvenience of living in a house whose most important room is temporarily "closed for remodeling."

LET'S START WITH YOUR FAMILY

HOW MANY SHARE IN THE COOKING?

You can design your kitchen to showcase the talents of a solo culinary virtuoso—or stage it for a whole ensemble of cooks. Once you decide if your kitchen is the domain of just one family member, or an arena for several chefs, you'll know just what to anticipate in arranging your work centers, allocating space, and choosing the kind and number of appliances to plug into your kitchen plan.

If your kitchen is primarily a workshop for only one person—or only one person at a time—then you can plan it with minimum dimensions, and without a lot of extra appliances or equipment. In fact, that's just what you should plan: most one-person kitchens become more efficient by tightening up the distances between the range, sink, and refrigerator. For some specific measurements that work, see page 64.

Here especially, give the solo cook a break by keeping through-kitchen traffic to a minimum. It's worth your efforts to plan your one-person kitchen so it's sidestepped by the family stampede. But that's not to say it has to put the cook in exile. As in the kitchen *at left,* a counter open to adjacent living areas can keep open the lines of communication—without lines of traffic.

Doubling up

If you have a helper when it's time to put dinner on the table at your house (or if you'd just like to encourage one), you should plan your kitchen for two. That doesn't necessarily mean that your kitchen needs twice the space of a one-cook version; a little more elbow room at the appliance work centers usually does the trick. If you opt for the maximum distances between these points on the kitchen work triangle, two cooks can work side by side without getting in each other's way.

In a corridor or galley kitchen where a triangular arrangement of work centers isn't always possible, make room for two cooks by widening the aisle between the two appliance walls.

Two cooks can't cook efficiently if one is always waiting in line to use an appliance, so

consider doubling up on some equipment. Perhaps your kind of kitchen creations demand a double-oven range and an extra sink—or maybe all the two of you will need is a larger cooktop and an extra cutting board. Let the kind of cooking you do help you decide.

The family that cooks together

The family that cooks together may give up on the idea if they're forever knocking elbows in the kitchen. To keep your kitchen crew efficient, willing, and civil, your first priority is to provide adequate aisle and counter space. And if that's just not possible in your present kitchen, you probably should consider annexing adjoining space (see pages 66 and 67) or adding on (see pages 68 and 69). Chapter 6—''Putting It All Together'' —offers tips on working with kitchen designers and architects, and on doing parts of the remodeling work yourself.

Next, set up and equip each kitchen work center independently of the others. If a cook at the baking center needs measuring cups, the only set in the kitchen shouldn't be across the room at the food-preparation center. Equipping each center with knives, measuring cups and spoons, mixing bowls, and a few other commonly used items means a larger investment in cookware and utensils, but it's the only way multiple cooks can work together smoothly. Chapter 8—''Stocking Your Kitchen''—will help you decide what frequently used kitchen tools you may need more of.

DO YOU NEED EATING SPACE?

Dining room dining was traditional in the days of butlers and serving girls, and it's still nice for special occasions. But today's families live more casually, often in less spacious homes, and definitely without a cadre of household help. So what always has been the most comfortable eating spot in the house is now also the most practical one. You guessed it: it's the kitchen table.

An eating space can help you make the most of your kitchen, but just what shape it takes depends on a number of factors.

How much space is enough?
Even if your kitchen isn't big enough for a conventional table and chairs, don't rule out kitchen dining until you've considered a snack counter or even a booth. There's information about sizing up your kitchen for both on page 76, and about general dining space requirements on page 75.

The table-and-chairs-size dining area shown here works fine for a family of four or five; a family much larger than that might do better with a kitchen eating spot geared to snacks and off-hour meals for just a few family members. Then they could reserve a more spacious area of the house for whole-family get-togethers.

Other considerations
Not the least advantage of an eat-in kitchen is the way it simplifies serving and clean-up chores. With ample counter space between the cooking and dining areas, you can prepare and serve meals all within the space of a few feet. And at the end of the meal, your clean-up center is no more than a few steps away—not off in another room.

There's also an undeniable appeal to eating in a room that's still permeated with all the tantalizing smells of food being prepared. On the other hand, some diners would willingly trade those scents for some visual distance from the pots and pans they emanate from. Is the sensory experience of kitchen dining worth looking at the clutter? It's a trade-off really, and a strictly personal decision.

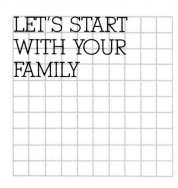
HOW MUCH TIME DOES YOUR FAMILY SPEND IN THE KITCHEN?

If the answer to the question above is "not much," maybe it's because your present kitchen doesn't give them anything to do there besides cooking and cleaning up afterward. Think of a friend's or neighbor's kitchen you especially enjoy visiting, and you'll probably realize that its appeal comes from the *other* things it offers—an informal place to sit down over a cup of coffee, to plan a week's grocery list, or to write a letter. If you want your kitchen to attract your family, make it a magnet for the things they like to do.

B eyond the normal food preparation chores, there are really just two reasons why anyone would want to spend their time in the kitchen: because it's where there's (a) something you want to do, or (b) someone you want to be with. With this in mind, here are some ideas for making your kitchen an activity center in its own right, and a comfortable place to socialize with the cook.

An open invitation
If that's the feeling you want your new kitchen to extend, there's no better way to promote it than with an open floor plan. Choose a layout that naturally directs traffic to—or even through—the kitchen (pages 64 and 65 show the six basic kitchen layouts and tell about how each handles traffic). And when the family's all there, you should be prepared with ample seating for them so they're close enough for conversation, but not in the cook's way (see pages 74-77 for information about chairs, stools, and bench seating).

Kids in the kitchen
Kids and kitchens have long been just about inseparable. At your house, the draw may be the smell of what's cooking, the beckoning refrigerator, or the simple fact that *you're* there a lot. Whatever the reason, it doesn't make sense to start a kitchen project without some thought to the young set.

Maybe you'll simply need to provide a table and chairs (or a counter with stools) to serve as an after-school landing pad where the kids can play back their day over a plate of cookies. Or if you'd like to encourage more active participation and launch the career of the next Julia Child or James Beard, you'll want to arrange

some cabinet storage at child height, or, at your discretion, provide a step stool to increase your kids' reaches.

Consider, too, that if there's anything that attracts children more readily than a kitchen, it's a TV set. Combining the two lets you keep an eye on the kids' viewing habits. The kitchen shown here includes a radio as well, along with a convenient planning center. (To learn about the ingredients for a successful planning center, see page 72.)

Diners, dawdlers, and doodlers
Of all the things you can incorporate into a kitchen, few are more versatile than a dining table and chairs. Of course, they provide comfortable seating for dining, but marry the table with storage for art supplies, books, or games, and you've got a craft center, a desk, and another family room in the bargain. For more ideas on getting your kitchen to do more, see Chapter 7—"What Else Could Your Kitchen Do?"

No trespassing
On the other hand, maybe you don't think togetherness is the greatest thing ever stirred up in your kitchen. If you're a nononsense cook who wants the work areas cleared of nonessentials, particularly nonworking family members, you'll want to plan your kitchen from a different angle.

Make sure traffic patterns avoid your kitchen's work areas completely, and tighten up the work center triangle so there's no room for loitering. Let other rooms of your house become the study, snack, and conversation areas.

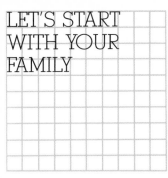

WHAT SORTS OF MEALS DO YOU PREPARE?

Is yours a family of culinary hobbyists always looking for new ways to use a food processor...or are you meat-and-potatoes cooks who, more often than not, eat and run? The kind of cooking you do says a lot about your family's version of the ideal kitchen —its layout, complement of appliances, and amount of storage. So look at what you cook and how, then customize your kitchen the way you season a recipe—until it's just right!

The kind of cooking you do determines a lot more than just the food you take to the table. It can—and should—determine the kind of kitchen that's best for you, in terms of equipment, storage, and dining and serving facilities. Here's a quick survey of variations on the cooking theme that will help you see where you and your ideal kitchen fit in.

The quantity cook
If meals at your house are prepared in camp-size quantities for a large family with appetites to match, space is your number-one kitchen consideration. Specifically, you'll need a large-capacity refrigerator for storing fresh foods (see Chapter 5—"Selecting Kitchen Components") and plenty of cabinet storage for oversize cookware, more tableware, and more grocery staples. (Chapter 9—"Details"—gives ideas for maximizing kitchen storage.)

Not only will you need more storage space, you'll need larger space, too, for oversize serving pieces such as platters, casseroles, and tureens.

The convenience cook
If you're sold on the virtues of convenience foods and whirlwind cooking, efficiency is your kitchen motto. Start with the most efficient floor plan you can (see pages 64 and 65), then augment it with extra storage space for packaged and frozen foods, a battery of small appliances, and if possible, a microwave oven. (Page 72 tells how to plan a microwave cooking center.)

The prepare-ahead cook
For the chef who specializes in preparing meals days in advance and squirreling them away for instant serving, again, appliances rate top priority. A large-capacity refrigerator is a must (and possibly a separate freezer, too), and for last-minute preparation, a microwave oven is almost as essential.

Since prepare-ahead cooks also tend to be super-efficient cooks, a kitchen layout with work centers in a tight, step-saving triangle is important, as are easily maintained surfaces on the floor, counters, and cabinets (see Chapter 3— "Face-Lifting a Kitchen").

The experimental cook
The experimental cook needs more of just about everything —more space, more storage (for specialized utensils and tableware), and more in the way of equipment. Concerning equipment, make sure that it's within easy reach; a food processor, a pasta maker, and an espresso machine are of little use if you can't get to them (see how to set up an "appliance garage" on page 136).

If your experiments include a lot of baking, by all means make room for a separate baking center in your kitchen. Page 73 tells how.

The business cook
If, more than just a pleasure, cooking is how you earn your bread and butter, you'll want a kitchen that functions just like what it is—a place of business. For instance, the man-about-the-kitchen shown here "retired" from the brokerage business to teach cooking. If you're thinking about teaching, catering, or baking to order, every kitchen center has to function at top efficiency. Plan for a floor covering that's comfortable underfoot for hours at a time, and surfaces that are attractive and easy to clean. Most important, don't skimp on kitchen lighting (see pages 142 and 143).

HOW DO
YOU SHOP?

Are you a city dweller who can make daily stops for fresh food at a variety of neighborhood shops? Or are you country folk who plan meals for weeks on end and, two or three times a month, make a big run on the supermarket? Even if you're not quite either, you can appreciate how different the storage and refrigeration needs of these two shoppers might be. And you can see how your shopping patterns can help shape the design of your kitchen.

There may be as many schools of thought on food shopping as there are on playing the stock market. One approach may be as valid as another, but each presents a different challenge when you sit down to plan your kitchen.

What do you find in your shopping cart? Mostly canned or frozen foods, lots of fresh produce, or some of each?

Canned versus fresh

If you prepare fresh foods more often than canned or frozen, you probably shop often, perhaps daily. And you rely heavily on your refrigerator. Since you make frequent shopping trips, you may get along nicely in a compact kitchen with relatively little storage space, mainly for staples.

The less often you shop, the more likely that what you bring home will be mostly canned and/or frozen foods. Again, your refrigerator is important—this time for its freezer capacity. But ample cabinet storage for canned goods is just as critical.

The food closet shown on these pages is customized for cans. Its shelves are adjustable, and they're shallow so packaged goods are never stored more than two deep. You'll find more kitchen storage ideas on pages 136-141.

The quantity shopper

It can be reassuring to shop for the proverbial rainy day, or to take advantage of special buys. The problem is finding a place to store all you bring home. If you know that you're a quantity shopper, plan as much storage space into your kitchen as you can. And look for more storage away from

your kitchen—in a pantry area or basement, for instance.

Consider not only the quantity of what you bring home, but its bulk as well. If you automatically reach for economy-size packages, reserve some kitchen storage for these behemoths (or for the large storage containers you transfer the foods into).

The light shopper

Small families, couples, and singles usually don't need a lot of food storage, but they may need specialized storage. For instance, a family of German shepherd fanciers will need plenty of space under the counter for 20-pound bags of dog food. And a single who eats on the run may need most of his or her storage space in the freezer—for serving-size frozen entrées—and on counter tops for convenience appliances like a toaster oven and a microwave.

For the family of whatever size that buys food in average quantities but only cooks it in small ones, plan your storage cabinets to handle yet-to-be-used food in jars or plastic containers (see page 138 for a convenient cupboard setup that does just that).

The cook-ahead shopper

How are the kitchen needs of the cook-ahead shopper different from those of the quantity shopper? Both bring home plenty of groceries, of course. But the bargain-hunting quantity shopper puts most of them right into storage; the person who cooks ahead uses them sooner, but has the prepared dishes to store. Where one needs more cabinet storage, the other needs refrigerator and freezer capacity (and perhaps room for a microwave cooking center to make the most of cook-ahead menus).

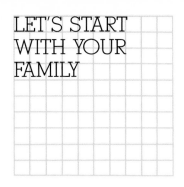
WHAT ARE PARTIES LIKE AT YOUR HOUSE?

Are they informal dinners for a few friends? Potlucks for the whole neighborhood? Something you look forward to once a year, or something that happens every weekend? The kind of parties you give can give something back to you—clues to some very helpful "extras" you should consider adding to your kitchen.

Your parties don't have to make the society page to have style—that ever-present intangible in the way you entertain that says *you.* If you've never given the subject much thought before, here's a good chance to see what your style has to say about your kitchen's design.

Strictly for kids

If most of your parties involve the younger set (kids up to age 10 or 11), you'll no doubt be on the guest list as supervising host or hostess. With kids in the kitchen, your motto should be "Keep it safe...and keep it clean." Make sure that knives, cleaning supplies, and breakables are out of reach (as well as, perhaps, the cookie jar). And plan surfaces with easy cleanup in mind. A refrigerator with a door that hides fingerprints (possibly outfitted with an in-door beverage dispenser) makes special sense

here. See Chapter 3—"Face-Lifting a Kitchen"—for more about easy-care surfaces, and pages 148 and 149 for tips on kitchen safety.

Teenagers, on the other hand, are quite capable of entertaining themselves, which they'll do best in a kitchen with an eating area or snack counter that can double as serving space for pizzas and snacks. With teenage appetites what they are, allow plenty of refrigerator storage for soft drinks and munchies.

Adults only

Maybe your parties are off limits to minors. In that case, you'll want to consider incorporating a bar/serving center in your kitchen. Pages 116 and 117 tell about wet bars and kitchen wine storage. If you entertain frequently, however, a kitchen wet bar may not be the best answer; you should consider taking bar-

tending duties out of the kitchen altogether and giving them house space all their own.

Since cocktail parties can involve specialized equipment—such as food warmers, chafing dishes, large hors d'oeuvre platters, and plenty of glassware—build adequate cabinet storage into your kitchen. The island shown *below left* adds cooking, storage, and serving facilities all at once.

Backyard gourmets

When the weather's nice, do you eat in your yard or on your patio or deck as much as you do in your kitchen? If yours is a family of outdoor enthusiasts when it comes to eating, try to think of outdoor areas as adjuncts to your kitchen. For instance, plan access to your patio from the kitchen, and arrange the two areas to allow an open flow of space. Not only will you enjoy your yard more, you'll simplify mealtime serving and cleanup.

Everyone in the act

Entertaining today is more relaxed than ever before, and so it's not uncommon to find everyone on the guest list out in the kitchen pitching in. To promote that kind of *esprit de corps,* you need a kitchen that's large enough to provide work space for several cooks at a time. Widen the distance between parallel counters, and arrange your "work triangle" of appliances with extra inches between stations. Check out the floor plans on pages 64 and 65 for layouts that work.

While you're planning, don't forget space for spectators. Provide sideline seating—counter stools or chairs at the kitchen table—for guests who want to join in the conversation but not the cooking. Pages 74-77 show several kitchen seating arrangements.

WHAT ABOUT CLEAN-UP CHORES?

One thing's for sure, they won't go away just by turning this page. But the few minutes you invest here reading about these less-than-popular kitchen duties will pay handsome dividends. You'll discover work-saving tips to help you plan the best kitchen arrangement, get the most from your appliances and equipment, and develop a clean-up routine that may leave you with newfound time to spare.

An ounce of prevention is worth a pound of cure may indeed be just another cliché, but when it comes to cleaning up a kitchen, it's one of the truisms of the age. The trick is to plan your kitchen to function well at the outset, then to develop work habits that keep cleanup to a minimum. If you succeed at these, the actual mop and bucket brigade will have lots less to complain about.

Planning—your biggest work saver

When do you use your kitchen clean-up center the most? Usually, it's when you're preparing food before a meal and when you're cleaning up afterward. So to save steps, design your kitchen to put the clean-up center *between* your food-preparation and serving/dining areas. This central location for your sink, dishwasher, and possibly trash compactor will do more to ease your cleaning load than any other design improvement you can make. See page 70 for more on setting up an efficient clean-up center.

Think about the surfaces in your kitchen, too. Easy-to-wipe-off counter tops, tabletops, and floors show their real beauty when it's time to clean them up. See Chapter 3—"Face-Lifting a Kitchen" —for a selection of the best in good-looking, easy-care surface materials.

Finally, help yourself by thinking "cleanup" each time you cook. Even a relatively simple choice of cookware (such as a nonstick pan) or recipe (a one-dish meal you can cook and serve in the same utensil, for instance) can mean a substantial savings of time and work.

Appliance helpers

Of all the appliances you can include in your kitchen, a dishwasher has the greatest potential for cutting your clean-up time. But to get the most from a dishwasher, study its owner's manual and follow its suggestions for loading the dish racks, the proper amounts of detergent and rinse agent to use, and any special pretreating requirements.

The same advance homework will sharpen the performance you get from two other valuable appliances—your waste disposer and trash compactor. Knowing what they can handle with ease, and what they were never designed to handle, will keep both high on the active list.

To save the time and mess of oven cleaning, consider a self-cleaning or perhaps a continuous-cleaning model. Microwave ovens, on the other hand, never require such heavy-duty cleaning—and they may even cut your dishwashing load by letting you cook and serve in the same dish, or on individual dinner plates.

There's more on choosing and using these and other appliances in Chapter 5—"Selecting Kitchen Components."

Products and procedures

Stock a good assortment of cleaning supplies and equipment at or near the kitchen sink (consider a locked cabinet for these supplies if you have small children). And when it comes time to use them, give some thought to ways you can make kitchen cleanup more orderly and efficient. For instance, use a rolling cart to bring dinner dishes from the table to the clean-up center all at once. Or store frequently used tableware and utensils near the dishwasher to simplify putting them away.

KITCHEN CLEAN-UP TIPS

Here are ways you can shortcut—or prevent—many common cleaning chores. For more clean-cut suggestions, see Chapter 10—"Kitchen Keeping."

Ounces of prevention

• Wipe up food spills on your range or cooktop as they happen, before they have a chance to bake on.
• Don't let gas flames lick the sides of your cookware; they cause heat stains.
• Use a spatter guard (or an inverted colander over the skillet) when you fry anything with popping grease, such as bacon or chicken.

How to avoid scouring

• Avoid cooking alkaline foods such as spinach or potatoes in aluminum cookware. It will darken the aluminum, making scouring necessary.
• If you need to boil eggs in an aluminum pan, add a little vinegar to the water to keep the aluminum from darkening.
• To remove burned or scorched food from the bottom of an aluminum pan, fill the pan with water and bring it to boiling. Then remove the softened food with a wooden spoon or pot scraper.
• To brighten aluminum cookware, use it to cook acidic foods, such as apples or rhubarb.
• To loosen food from enamel cookware, fill the utensil with cold water and let it stand until the food is softened.

• For food burned onto enamel cookware, fill the pot or pan with a water and baking soda solution (2 teaspoons soda per quart of water) and bring it to boiling. The food will loosen enough to be removed with a scraper or plastic sponge.
• Remove stains or cloudiness from glassware by filling glasses with water to which a teaspoon or two of ammonia has been added. Let stand for several hours or overnight, then rinse thoroughly.
• To whiten a porcelain sink, fill it with lukewarm water, add a little chlorine bleach, and let it stand for a short time.
• Rinse egg dishes with cold water. Extremely hot water will cook the eggs to the surface, making them difficult to remove.
• For burned spots on glass ceramic cookware, fill utensils with a water and baking soda solution and let it stand.

Penny-wise but pound-foolish

• Don't store leftover food in metal or enamel cookware. Salt and acids in the food could damage the utensils.
• Don't soak glassware with gilt or silver ornamentation in hot water. The decoration can soak off if the water is too hot or if the glassware is left in warm suds for too long.
• Don't run cold water into hot cookware. It can warp metal pans, or crack glass or earthenware.

HOW CAN YOU CONSERVE KITCHEN ENERGY?

Mention energy conservation and the first things most people think of are setting back thermostats, turning off lights, and perhaps adding insulation. But saving energy doesn't end with obvious strategies like these. For instance, just within your kitchen, the kind of appliances you choose—and how you use them—can do more to lower your overall power bill than you might imagine.

It's no secret that appliances can save us plenty of human energy in the kitchen. But did you know that you can help your appliances save you fuel energy, too—by choosing them with care, installing them properly, and using them with an eye to cutting operating costs? The kitchen *opposite* is a perfect example —from its energy-efficient fluorescent lights (behind translucent diffuser panels) right on down to its battery of energy-saving appliances.

Look for the label

Whenever you shop for a major appliance, look for the bright yellow Energy-Guide label. It's required by law on all refrigerators, freezers, dishwashers, washers, water heaters, room air conditioners, and home furnace systems.

The label is designed to show you at a glance how a particular model compares to others in terms of energy use and cost of operation. If an appliance is available powered by either gas or electricity, the label gives you figures for both. It also lists the capacity and features of the particular model, and an estimate of its yearly cost of operation based on a national average energy rate. For comparison purposes, the lowest and highest yearly operating costs for comparable models produced by competing manufacturers are also given. By studying the Energy-Guide label on an appliance, you can find out exactly what you're getting—and what you can expect to spend on energy.

The energy-efficient refrigerator

Since the refrigerator may be the single biggest energy-user in your kitchen, it makes sense to minimize its energy con-sumption any way you can. To begin with, choose a model with efficient cabinet and door insulation (possibly one with an in-door beverage or ice dispenser to minimize loss of cooled air by frequent door openings). Then locate your refrigerator away from your range or other heat-producing appliances, and out of direct sunlight. Settings of 40° F in the refrigerator section and 0° F in the freezer maximize energy efficiency.

You'll also save energy by using your refrigerator wisely. Cool hot foods slightly before refrigerating them. Check periodically that door seals are tight and condenser coils clean. And most important, open the door as quickly and infrequently as possible.

The energy-efficient dishwasher

Since an automatic dishwasher uses less hot water (and energy to heat it) than washing and rinsing dishes by hand, any dishwasher can save you money on energy. But to compound your energy savings, look for these other features when you shop.

An appliance with a large capacity will let you accumulate a full day's worth of dishes so you only have to put the dishwasher through its paces once a day. And look for a model with a self-cleaning built-in filter so you can avoid prerinsing your dishes and also prevent food particles from recirculating in the water.

Some models feature a low-energy wash cycle, and a low-energy drying cycle that lets dishes air-dry without the heating element. (To let dishes air-dry, you also can manually turn off your dishwasher before the drying cycle begins.)

Since most dishwashers need 140° F hot water for effi-cient operation, check to see that your home's hot water heater is set high enough, but not higher than necessary. On some dishwashers, you can get by with a lower hot water heater setting because the machine preheats incoming water to the necessary temperature.

Energy-efficient cooking

When it comes to cooking, the kinds of foods you cook and how you cook them can have as great an impact on energy consumption as the efficiency of the appliances you choose. For instance, you'll come out ahead if you prepare several dishes at once and can cook a whole meal in the oven at the same time. Or if you just need to cook a single baked potato, use a toaster oven instead of your conventional oven.

When you choose a new oven, look for models with as much insulation as possible. Those with high-heat or "pyrolitic" self-cleaning ovens already will have extra insulation, boosting their energy efficiency for regular cooking. Also consider a microwave oven for saving cooking energy. It uses considerably less electricity than a conventional electric oven, and doesn't heat up the kitchen, which can save air-conditioning energy.

Energy-efficient cooking on your cooktop or range depends a lot on your cooking habits. Keep pots and pans covered while food is cooking to minimize heat loss, and use the lowest heat setting recommended in the recipe. Use flat-bottomed pots and pans to more evenly distribute heat to cooking foods, and for greatest efficiency, adjust your gas burner flame to match the size of pan you're using.

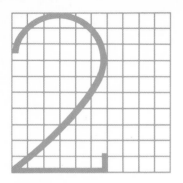

WHAT'S YOUR STYLE?

A kitchen can be attractive, colorful, even well-decorated, and still lack style. Why? Because all its separate components don't contribute to a total effect, a *feeling*. And that's basically what style is all about —creating a special feeling or atmosphere.

Each distinct style has characteristic elements —materials, surfaces, patterns, textures, and colors—that combine for a particular ambience. The next 20 pages introduce you to these basic ingredients, and tell how you can achieve the style that's right for you.

Let's start our style survey with an analysis of one of today's most popular looks—country. Probably the first thing that strikes you about country is its warmth and charm. This is a friendly, inviting, comfortable way to go. A country-style kitchen looks like it's been filled with generations of family living and love. You can almost smell the sweet aroma of corn bread baking in a wood-fired oven. Nostalgia? Perhaps, but a reverence for times past plays a major role in a kitchen that's gone country.

What do you need to gain this down-home effect?

Go back to nature

Wood, stone, brick, quarry tile—these are the natural, earthy elements that start your country-style decorating in the right direction.

The cozy kitchen dining area shown here takes on at least a century in age and seems far from the nearest city, thanks to a rough-cut stone fireplace wall, natural wood on the ceiling and lower wall, and furniture crafted of rugged American oak.

The best colors for country styling come from nature, too. You can't miss with deep, rich berry colors such as blue, burgundy, and plum. Or use earthy garden colors of golden corn and sun-warmed pumpkins.

Play up the handcrafted look

Part of country's appeal comes from the self-sufficiency of rural settlers. Now the products of their independent life-style re-create the essence of country in decorating.

Hand-loomed fabric—either real or commercially simulated —provides the look you want at windows or for seat cushions. Shop for rough weaves, knotted surfaces, and interesting textures.

Braided or hooked rugs add still more country-crafting to your kitchen. And don't overlook woven baskets, handhewn wood pieces, or earthen crocks that look like they've "put down" decades' worth of pickles and kraut.

Make the most of metals

Country living, as it inspires current decorating trends, definitely predates plastic. So for sparkling accents with rural authenticity, plan to include items of burnished copper or brass, pewter, cast iron, even speckled enamelware. And look for things that, by function—or at least appearance—are throwbacks to an earlier era. (On the next two pages you'll find detailed information on country accessories, what to look for, and where to find them.)

Our country kitchen *at right* has as its focal point a magnificent old blue enamel cookstove. Prowl the antique shops in your area and you may discover other characteristically country finds.

Pick your patterns carefully

There are, of course, some historic patterns that are always right in a country setting. One of them is the Blue Willow tableware shown here. Even without a specific, time-honored design, you still can be on target if you select a small geometric print, or an informal floral pattern, perhaps one that hints of wildflowers strewn across a country meadow.

SELECTING COUNTRY ACCESSORIES

The final—and most powerful—stroke in countrifying your kitchen happens when you add the accessories. But choosing pieces that are just "nice and old" doesn't get the job done. You need to think "country" all the way, and choose accessories —some decorative, some still useful—that would have been practical items in a rural home a century ago.

Putting country in your kitchen means transplanting yourself, mentally, back to a different time and life-style. Look at what country living was really like, then pick up remnants of that past to use as decorative items in your kitchen.

Tools of the times
Though we wouldn't trade our electric lights for oil lamps, or our cars for Old Dobbin, vestiges of that earlier life make ideal decorating accessories.

Look for things such as horse brasses or other bits of tack, cow bells, milk cans and pails, hand tools, oil lamps, candlesticks, and wooden storage boxes.

Most of these items are readily available at auctions, garage and estate sales, and antique shops.

Weathervanes seem symbolic of country living and provide some examples of exquisite folk art in metal. Use them as wall pieces or mount them on wood blocks as sculpture. But be prepared to pay investment prices for these sought-after collectibles.

Kitchen memorabilia
If you think back to the woodstove era, you'll come up with dozens of handsome kitchen utensils that are perfect as flavor-makers for your country kitchen. Use everything from baking pans and cookware to metal storage boxes, canning equipment, and kitchen tools.

Mellow old copper pots are natural country charmers. In the room *above, left,* an oversize cooking pot is ready to go

to work on a hearty stew. Notice the open shelves displaying more copper, baskets, and country crockery.

And don't overlook the obvious. Baskets were a big part of our country cousins' lives. Vegetables were harvested, flowers picked, sewing and mending stored—all in various, interesting baskets.

The kitchen *opposite* gives a good idea of the decorating impact you can get from baskets alone. Against the area's white boards and brick, the natural-colored baskets exude a golden warmth.

Tableware helps along the country look, too. Choose pewter plates and goblets, heavy ironstone dishes, or speckled enamelware.

In the kitchen *above, right,* interestingly shaped utensils hang from the underside of a mantel, and a set of pewter measures is arrayed along the top. More pewter graces the table.

Leisure-time leftovers
Country kids obviously didn't watch TV, so their fun-time pursuits have left us with some whimsical rural-life accents. Keep your eyes open for old wind toys, wooden toys, and game boards.

Winter evening hobbies also produced examples of folk art paintings, embroidery, and quilting that convert easily to kitchen accessories with a country air about them.

Do-it-yourself accents
For more country atmosphere, try stenciling your floor or walls, adding a chair rail or wainscot—or even adding an old-timey tin ceiling, available again, often from original manufacturers.

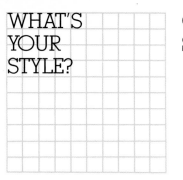
CITY SLICK

The flip side of the country decorating coin is this cool, restrained, efficient look. It's often characterized as "high tech," but we call it "city slick." Of course you're just as free to try it in suburbia or on an acreage. In this brave new world of kitchen styling, what's decorative gets used and what's used becomes decorative. City slick is as close to the modernist credo of "form follows function" as kitchens have ever come. Function fathers the whole decorating style.

The secret to city slick is honest, straightforward use of space and materials. Here, an appliance, cooking utensil, or can of soup is just that. You don't have to hide or cover up. In fact, city slick depends heavily on open shelves, glass cases, and vinyl-coated wire racks for both storage and display of functioning elements. The version shown here even uses a chain-link gate, ceiling-hung, for convenient storage of good-looking cooking gear.

Be straight about materials
For this kind of high-style look, you have to maintain an equally high standard of material integrity. Let wood stay natural in color—don't attempt to camouflage metal—and use vinyls, acrylics, and other plastics for their innate beauty and function.

Color, pattern, and such
White seems to be an odds-on favorite for this no-frills style, though when colors are used, they're usually strong, often primary hues.

Patterns are virtually nonexistent in city slick, unless they appear as geometric designs in the installation of floor or wall tiles.

Window treatments have gone by the way, too. The most appropriate look here is an undecorated window, though mini-slat blinds are also compatible with the frankly functional look of city slick.

Just because a kitchen focuses on function doesn't mean it has to look bleak and industrial. Add an interesting touch here and there to soften the effect. Use plants, baskets, even an antique or two. Just keep these purely accessory items to a minimum.

CONTEMPORARY

Loosely defined, "contemporary" means "of the present time." But the true beauty of contemporary design is that it's timeless. This enduring style goes from decade to decade without dating itself, as less-classic looks might. Why the timelessness of good contemporary styling? One word—simplicity. In its classic beauty, a kitchen featuring this understated, carefully executed style is like a Japanese flower arrangement, which never has more than a few absolutely perfect blooms. Contemporary is restrained, simple, flawless in detail and arrangement, with a beauty that goes well beyond "of the present time."

The shape of things is important in a contemporary environment. As you can see by the curvilinear kitchen on these pages, materials and shape play a larger part than surface decoration.

Colors and patterns
Colors in this decorating style are bold, strong, and pure; no weak pastels, thanks. For the most powerful effect, bounce hefty colors off plenty of white. Patterns need to have a solid foundation in contemporary styling. As a cover-up or a superficial treatment for walls, pattern just isn't valid. On the other hand, pattern is right at home if it's born of geometry in the installation of tiles, wood, or other structural material. For instance, the brilliant blue tile floor in this kitchen gives both pattern and color to a scheme otherwise too hard-edged.

The material difference
A contemporary kitchen is the natural place for today's most exciting new materials. Use plastics, vinyls, high-shine chrome, and clear glass.

Accessories, too, need to be distinctive. Some of your best bets are handcrafted ceramics, wood or metal sculpture, and graphics. Prints under glass add a unique character to any style of kitchen. But use accessories sparingly; arrange a few simple pieces in a grouping, or place one important object so it relates well to the space around it.

And don't be afraid to under-decorate your contemporary kitchen. It's perfectly all right to leave walls blank, windows bare, and some breathing room around objects on your counter tops.

31

GREEN
AND
GROWING

Houseplants just may be the most burgeoning decorating trend ever to hit today's kitchen styling. And why not? Plants are a complete decorating package you can put together by the potful. With their lush, green foliage or bright blossoms, plants provide both color and texture —or in the case of a windowsill herb garden, flavor as well. They're the room's naturally perfect accessories, yet at the same time, they can be arranged to become its focal interest. In a kitchen, well-placed plants soften the rigid lines of cabinets and appliances. And for general atmosphere, nothing beats the lighthearted, natural look of a "planted" kitchen.

A green thumb helps, certainly, but it's not the most important requisite for this fresh, informal kitchen style. What's essential is a genuine love of plants as living things—not simply decorative accessories. If you've got that, the rest is a cinch.

Where does your garden grow?

Here, room-spanning shelves under spacious skylights provide a natural environment for greenery. In another kitchen plants might have to settle for space on the windowsills, on wall-mounted shelves, or in ceiling-hung slings—wherever they get the best possible light. (More about this on the next two pages.)

Plants as design elements

Avoid monotony in the staging of your plants: vary their sizes and shapes. Also vary their "characters" by including some stalky, treelike plants, and others that climb or drape.

Group several plants into a single arrangement. It's more attractive than spacing them evenly along a shelf or windowsill.

Don't skimp on the number of plants you use. If you're creating the garden look in your kitchen, you can't do it with a few small pots of violets.

Background and containers

Plants in effect make their own limelight when you feature them against a light background that won't detract from their color and texture. And to keep your plants visually "stage center," be sure to pot them in neutral or subtly colored containers. That way your eye focuses on the blooms and foliage, not on a hodgepodge of brightly colored pots.

PLANTS FOR KITCHEN GARDENS

The success of a green and growing kitchen depends on keeping it that way. Light, temperature and humidity, food and water—any plant owes its very life to the environment and care you provide.

Fortunately, there's nothing really mysterious about a plant's needs. You simply choose the right species for the light levels available at your house, water on schedule, and master a few other horticultural basics.

Light

Of all plant needs, light is clearly the most critical. First, consider your kitchen's exposures. Usually you can expect to get the best growing light from south, east, and west windows—in that order. Of course, trees outside, a large roof overhang, and nearby houses also can affect the amount of light plants receive.

Next, determine how much light experts recommend for your plant's species. Light requirements are usually expressed in relative terms, such as "low," "medium," or "high." What, specifically, do these mean? To find out, measure the distance between your kitchen windows and the spots you're planning for your plants. *Low* light levels occur six or more feet from an unshaded window; *medium,* three to six feet; *high,* two to three feet; and *very high,* closer than two feet.

Realize, too, that you can augment natural light with artificial light, both fluorescent and incandescent. Ultraviolet "plant" lights work best, but even ordinary incandescent bulbs and fluorescent tubes help in many situations.

Temperature and humidity

Most plants do best at room temperatures ranging from 50 to 85 degrees Fahrenheit, with no extreme changes or strong drafts. Flowering plants are especially susceptible to chills, which means you may need to close curtains at night.

Most houseplants come from the tropics, and prefer humidity levels of 30 to 40 percent. In the winter, household humidity can drop to 10 percent or less. Be on the alert to make up the difference. Add moisture to the air with a humidifier, or mist plants in the morning and/or early afternoon. Don't mist at night, though; damp leaves could rot.

Water and food

Generally, you should add water when the topsoil begins to feel dry, and water on a regular schedule. Plants in small pots require more frequent waterings than those in large pots, and flowering plants require more moisture than foliage plants. Just remember that when you water, do it thoroughly so that you moisten the soil all the way to the bottom of the pot.

Feeding needs fluctuate with the season of the year, as well as with the age and general health of your plants. Always read instructions on plant food packages, learn your plants' growth cycles, and feed accordingly.

The chart *at right* summarizes light and moisture needs for two popular categories of kitchen plants—flowering and foliage plants. Herbs and vegetables are discussed on pages 120 and 121.

KITCHEN PLANT NEEDS

	LIGHT	WATER
FLOWERING PLANTS		
African violet	High	Keep moist at all times.
Azalea	High to very high	Keep evenly moist.
Begonia	High	Let dry out slightly between waterings.
Bromeliad	High	Keep cup in center of plant filled.
Cyclamen	High	Keep evenly moist.
Fuchsia	High to very high	Keep evenly moist.
Geranium	High to very high	Let dry out slightly between waterings.
Gloxinia	High	Keep evenly moist.
Impatiens	Medium	Keep evenly moist.
Primrose	High	Keep evenly moist.
FOLIAGE PLANTS		
Airplane plant	High	Water when soil dries out.
Asparagus fern	Medium to high	Keep evenly moist.
Aspidistra (cast-iron plant)	Low	Keep evenly moist.
Baby's-tears	Medium to high	Keep evenly moist.
Cactus	High to very high	Water sparsely in winter.
Caladium	Medium to high	Keep evenly moist.
Chinese evergreen	Low to medium	Keep barely moist at all times.
Croton	High to very high	Keep evenly moist.
Dieffenbachia	Low to medium	Water when soil becomes dry.
Dracena	Medium to high	Keep evenly moist.
English ivy	Medium	Keep evenly moist.
Fern	Medium	Keep evenly moist.
Fiddle-leaf fig	Medium to high	Keep evenly moist.
German and Grape ivy	Low	Keep evenly moist.
Jade plant	Medium	Keep evenly moist except in winter.
Norfolk Island pine	Low to medium	Keep evenly moist.
Palm	High to very high	Water heavily except in winter.
Peperomia	Low to medium	Water sparingly.
Philodendron	Medium	Keep evenly moist.
Pick-a-back plant	Medium to high	Keep evenly moist.
Pothos	High	Water when soil becomes dry.
Purple velvet	Very high	Keep evenly moist.
Sansevieria	Low	Keep soil on the dry side.
Strawberry Saxifraga	High	Water when soil becomes dry.
String-of-pearls	Very high	Water when soil becomes dry.
Swedish ivy	Medium to high	Keep evenly moist.
Zebra plant	Very high	Keep evenly moist.

COLONIAL

A colonial kitchen—a genuine 1700s kitchen —wouldn't appeal very much to any of us. Who really wants to cook in the fireplace of a one-room house? Instead, to-day's colonial kitchen captures the warmth and charming "worn look" we like to asso-ciate with the era of our colonists—an adaptation that's far more livable than the real thing.

Though a colonial kitchen as we know it is a far cry from Martha Washing-ton's, there's still authenticity in how we arrive at this comfort-able design style.

Native woods, for instance, were the backbone of a colo-nist's existence. And mellow pine and warm, cheery maple are still the favorites for this look today.

The kitchen *at left* is perme-ated with colonial flavor, thanks to honey-colored cabi-nets, metal strap hinges, and white ceramic pulls. And there's more native wood in the sturdy ceiling beams and wide, flat window molding.

Colonial color and pattern
Since all fabrics used by the colonists had to be hand-dyed from natural materials, there are no strong, bright tones in a colonial kitchen. Instead, use muted, grayed, or natural col-ors as window treatments or fabric accents.

Average colonists didn't have access to the fine printed papers used by the aristocra-cy, so walls are most authentic if they're painted off-white to simulate plain, plastered sur-faces. Either leave them un-decorated or accent with hand-painted stencils (or sten-ciled-looking wall coverings) in Early American designs.

Accessories and how to use them
Here's where the colonial style really takes on its character. Choose decorative—or func-tional—pieces of copper, pew-ter, iron, wood, or woven rush. And plan to display utensils by hanging them from hooks at-tached to walls or mounted un-der your top cabinets.

37

ECLECTIC

To achieve an eclectic look, you can use absolutely anything you like. There are no strict boundaries to cramp your style. So what keeps an eclectic kitchen from becoming a jumbled mess of odds and ends? Here's the fine print on this decorating policy: the elements of eclectic styling are completely your choice—the arrangement, however, follows some clearly defined decorating principles.

The term "eclectic" actually means "made up of elements from various sources," which helps explain why this is such a popular and successful decorating style. Eclectic gives you a chance to do what you like, do as much or as little as you like, and live with all the things that are closest to your heart.

A matter of materials

The materials, surfaces, and equipment for your eclectic kitchen can be whatever you want. This is a great place to use hand-me-downs, second-hand store finds, and other recycled items. It's the intriguing mix of diverse designs and materials that makes this style so much fun.

And don't be afraid to combine old and new as in the kitchen *at right*. Under the leaded window, a new streamlined sink cabinet and counter top are sandwiched between an old oak-doored cabinet and a freestanding range.

Color and pattern

Color is an important part of any decorating scheme. The same is true in your eclectic kitchen. There's no restriction on the color you choose, its intensity, or its variations. But do make sure your room has the feeling of a dominant color or color family. Let one or two colors set the scene; otherwise you'll have a dizzying kaleidoscope of colors and no sense of order.

With pattern, again, anything goes. Use a little pattern, use a bundle of it—or none at all. If you combine several patterns within the kitchen, however, keep a thread of continuity. Make sure all relate to one another by way of a mutual color element or design, or a commonality in size.

TRADITIONAL

Not all of our past revolved about the tough struggle for existence suffered by average colonists, or the determined self-sufficiency of young rural America. Much of our heritage, certainly our European roots, included people accustomed to living in gracious, elegant surroundings. That life-style comes down to us as traditional—a look that speaks of refinement and exquisite taste. If you're a person who likes nice things, a sense of preeminence, and order, this ambience is for you.

Traditional is a bit more formal than colonial, and a lot more formal than country decorating. This look depends on fine woods and fine cabinetry, embellished with handsome detailing and ornate hardware.

The kitchen *at right* shows just how highly polished traditional can be. Graceful beams overhead, paneled doors and drawers, columnar corner posts on the base cabinets, even a metal bas-relief beneath the center island—just about every element harks back to a more elegant era.

Modern-day materials in traditional dress

In case you're wondering whether all the fittings here are antiques or costly custom-mades, most are neither. Just about every item is a stock component. The difference is that they were ordered from a catalog of bar/restaurant fixtures. That comfortably curved molding around the counter tops, for instance, would normally cradle drinkers' elbows; the foot-rail below is a standard saloon item, too. In fact, just about the only true antiques here are the ornate relief end panels on the island and the black-and-white etched glass insets.

Traditional colors and fabrics

You have just one restriction here: do not use strong, pure colors. They're characteristic of contemporary environments. Instead, pick rich, deepened colors that look as if they've aged for a century or two.

Fabrics can range from checked gingham to sumptuous damasks, toiles, and crewel-embroidered designs. Today's reproductions offer these looks in twentieth-century, easy-to-maintain fabrics.

ANTIQUE

Antiquity has its charm, but let's face it: no one wants to be a purist about antiquity in a kitchen. We simply aren't ready to give up our work-whittling appliances and easy-to-maintain surfaces. Yet we can create a compatible environment for our favorite antique pieces and, ultimately, have a kitchen that *looks* antique, yet functions like its best contemporary counterpart.

There's no way you're going to make a microwave oven or trash compactor look antique. So the answer to "How do I create an antique kitchen?" is simply this: simulate the walls and floor of an eighteenth-century house, load the area and its adjacent spaces with antique furniture and accessories, and you'll never be bothered that your kitchen isn't 100 percent antique. The total effect—which is what matters—will definitely belong to the 1700s.

First the walls

The right milieu for your antique collectibles is one that's as close to the original as possible. In the case of the kitchen dining area shown here, eighteenth-century furniture and accessories have dictated the simple white walls and chair rail of our early New England colonists.

You'll also notice that this dining area has a flat board with pegs wall-mounted near the ceiling. Its original use may have been for clothes or lanterns; now it displays favorite accessories. Pieces that normally sit on—or crowd—tabletops turn into an interesting wall grouping with this easy-to duplicate "peg" board.

Next, the floor

This kitchen sports wide pine planks, worn to a beautiful softness. Typical of a 1700s house, this look is not impossible to duplicate. Though the planks in this kitchen are honestly two hundred years old,

you'd be surprised at the aging process that can take place by "distressing" and staining new boards. For the sake of easy care, you may want to finish wood (either new or antique) with polyurethane varnish.

You needn't insist on wood underfoot, though. Bricks, slate, and quarry tiles also contribute to an antique mood. Or, for late twentieth-century ease of installation and maintenance, select modern-day resilient flooring with a brick or stone pattern. (There's more about all of these materials and how they compare in the chapter that follows.)

A guide to antique accessories

Anyone who collects antiques doesn't need to be told what to acquire—or, necessarily, where to use them. But for anyone who likes the antique *look* and wants to re-create it, here are the types of accessories to look for:

• Items made of tin, such as candle sconces, candlesticks, or utensils.

• Baskets of all sizes and shapes.

• Wooden boxes, tools, and toys.

• Tableware and serving pieces of pewter, yellowware, or Bennington pottery.

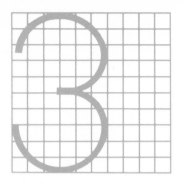

FACE-LIFTING A KITCHEN

Is your kitchen tired but still basically serviceable? If so, a few cosmetic changes can give it an entirely new personality. Walls and ceilings, floors, counter tops, and cabinets all lend themselves to relatively low-budget spruce-ups. This chapter zeros in on each of those surfaces, tells what your options are, and how you can coordinate them for the fresh new look you want.

Nothing punches up a kitchen more dramatically than a different wall and ceiling treatment. The photos *opposite* illustrate just a few of the myriad effects you can achieve. Whatever your choice, just remember that it has to stand up to grease, moisture, heat, and scrubbing. With these requirements in mind, let's survey the possibilities here, and again in chart form on pages 46 and 47.

The allure of paint
Check out the rich, green breakfast nook shown *opposite, upper right*, and you can see how a simple paint job can wake up a ho-hum room or area. In most instances, paint is the least expensive way to go—and the easiest.

Do bear in mind, though, that painting a kitchen, even a relatively small one, takes more time and patience than you'd need for other rooms; cutting in around cabinets, windows, and doors calls for lots of careful brushwork.

Don't try to economize on paint quality, either. Buy a good, tough gloss or semi-gloss paint or enamel. Flat finishes are too difficult to clean, and stains penetrate them more readily.

When you're selecting colors, don't rely on the small samples provided by the store. Instead, pick two or three colors that seem close to the one you want, purchase a half pint of each, and spread them out over foot-square areas. Let the paint dry thoroughly before you make your final decision; paints often lighten as they dry.

Dressing up with wall coverings
Looking for pattern and zip? Today's wall coverings offer choices galore. And they

needn't stick solely to walls, either. The kitchen *opposite, below* demonstrates how a plaid print can pull down a too-tall ceiling.

Most of the wall coverings best suited to the high humidity and scrubbing requirements of kitchens are either pure vinyl or other materials—such as paper and cloth—that have been coated with vinyl. Uncoated papers, delicate fabrics, and textured coverings such as burlap and grass cloth just don't hold up in cooking zones.

If your walls have surface defects, choose a textured or patterned covering that will conceal the blemishes. If your walls are smooth, or if you're willing to patch or plaster them back to health, also consider the more revealing, open effects of foil or wet-look vinyl.

Paneling for permanence
Paneling generally costs more than paint or paper, but once you've made the initial investment, it's there for the life of your kitchen.

You can choose paneling in a variety of price ranges and looks, including real and simulated wood, pattern-printed surfaces, and planks—like the ones applied diagonally to the shelf wall pictured *opposite, upper left.*

Accenting with ceramic tile
Though expensive, tile is worth the cost in areas where you need its durability and easy-wipe cleanability. And even a relatively small number of tiles can set the style for your entire kitchen.

Tiles work especially well as a backsplash for a counter top, or as a wipe-clean wall surface between a range and an exhaust hood.

(continued)

FACE-LIFTING
A KITCHEN

**WALLS
AND
CEILINGS**
(continued)

YOUR WALL AND CEILING OPTIONS

	TYPES	EFFECTS
PAINT	**Water-base (latex)** **Alkyd** **Urethane** **Polyurethane** **Epoxy**	Finishes range from absolutely flat to super-high gloss. Standard colors include an astonishing range of hues. You also can custom-mix just about any color you want. Specialty paints and additives let you achieve a low- to moderate-profile texture that looks much like plastered surfaces.
WALL COVERINGS	**Paper-backed vinyl** **Cloth-backed vinyl** **Wet-look vinyl** **Foil**	Myriad styles, patterns, and colors can highlight architectural details or make them disappear, establish an overall color scheme, or set a pattern motif. Some types come prepasted with an adhesive coating that saves you time and effort; others are strippable—you can remove them without steaming or scraping. Many coverings are machine-printed on high-speed presses; a few are printed by hand.
PANELING	**Plywood** **Solid planks** **Hardboard** **Plastic laminate**	Paneling achieves a natural-wood warmth with wood veneers of almost any species, or planking such as barn boards or tongue-and-groove boards. Printed hardboard also offers color and design motifs. Plastic laminates give color and sleekness, or the effect of butcher block, grass cloth, marble, and other materials.
TILE	**Ceramic** **Mosaic** **Resilient** **Brick** **Mirror** **Cork**	Ceramic tiles typically measure 4¼ or 6 inches square, but you can choose many other sizes and shapes; mosaics are smaller and usually are bonded to 1x1- or 1x2-foot mesh. Both come either glazed or unglazed in a broad range of colors, and—in some cases—hand-painted designs. Resilient tiles are a flooring material that works just as well on walls. Thin tiles of brick veneer, mirror, and cork let you achieve special effects.

DURABILITY	USES	INSTALLATION	COST
The higher the gloss, the longer a paint will last and the easier it will be to maintain. Flat latex surfaces smudge easily, and are the most difficult to clean. Epoxy and the urethanes are the toughest.	Latex and alkyd go on both primed or previously painted surfaces. Urethane and polyurethane can be applied to almost any surface. Epoxy won't adhere to painted surfaces; save it for covering or touching up tile, glass, or porcelainized items such as appliances and sinks.	One gallon typically covers about 400 square feet with one coat. Latex is the easiest to work with, alkyd slightly more difficult. Epoxy, which requires that you carefully mix two liquids, is the most difficult of all.	Cost varies according to the amount of gloss and degree of pigmentation; shinier surfaces and rich, deep colors generally cost more. Latex is usually the least expensive, followed by alkyd, the urethanes, and epoxy.
Wall coverings labeled "scrubbable" can withstand repeated washings. They will let you remove grease and smoke stains without damaging the wall covering's surface. Paper-backed vinyls can be wiped clean with a damp cloth. Don't use uncoated papers in a kitchen.	Most apply over any clean, sound surface, but if your walls are already covered with vinyl, you'll need to steam or strip it off first. With foils and wet-look vinyl, put up lining paper first to smooth out imperfections.	Rolls all cover 36 square feet, although the width may vary from 20½ to 28 inches; plan on getting 30 usable square feet per roll. Prepasted coverings are easiest to work with, hand-prints and foils the most difficult.	Prices vary widely, depending largely upon colors and patterns. Typically, hand-printed coverings and foils are the most costly; machine-printed paper the least.
If not protected with several coats of polyurethane, plywood and planks soak up kitchen grease. Hardboard is easier to maintain in high-soil areas; plastic laminate, the easiest of all.	The ideal cover-up for badly deteriorated walls; even bad bulges and bows can be evened out by first putting up furring strips. Moldings hide joints at any place where paneling abuts another surface or architectural element.	All but planks come in 4x8-foot sheets. Figure on one panel for every 4 linear feet of wall; unless the wall is mostly windows, doors, or cabinets, don't deduct for openings. Some types of paneling install with glue only; others require glue and nails.	Printed hardboard is usually the most economical; plywood and plank costs vary widely, depending on grade and species; plastic laminate is moderate, though bright solid colors and leathery textures can be costly.
Properly installed, ceramic and mosaic have the permanence of stone, though grout joints between the tiles may need to be cleaned and sealed periodically. Brick and mirror tiles are long-lasting, too; cork only moderately so.	Glazed ceramic and mosaic tiles are ideal for moist or frequently cleaned surfaces; unglazed tiles may need to be sealed. Don't use resilient, brick, mirror, or cork tiles in high-soil areas.	Measure carefully for tile, taking into account any trim pieces you may need to negotiate corners and round off edges. Add 10 percent to estimates to allow for cutting and waste. Resilient, brick, mirror, and cork tiles are easy to install. Ceramic tile is moderately difficult; grouting requires time and patience.	Ceramic and mosaic are moderate to expensive, depending on size, color, and type; materials to set tile run up the bill, as does, especially, trim. Other types of tile are moderate in cost.

FACE-LIFTING A KITCHEN

FLOORS

The floor—your kitchen's foundation—takes wear and tear, soil and spills that few other surfaces have to stand up to. Clearly, any face-lifting here has to be more than skin deep. And since flooring constitutes one of the largest uninterrupted surfaces in most kitchens, the type you select sets the decorating tone for the rest of the room. Fortunately, durability is built into all of today's popular materials, and style choices abound.

Selecting new flooring is a juggling act. Appearance, cleanability, comfort, acoustics, ease of installation, cost—no one material scores well in every single department (though a few come close). Here's an overview of the four major categories. A chart on the following pages tells more about your flooring options.

Natural wood: at home with any look

Wood flooring makes a rich background for any decorating scheme. It's equally at ease in an authentic traditional setting, or a crisply contemporary kitchen like the one pictured *opposite, below.*

Most wood floorings are equally tough, but differ in species, appearance, and price. You can choose narrow strips, wider planks, blocks, or parquet configurations.

Before you rush off to the lumberyard, though, consider that cleaning and maintaining a wood floor can be a pain in the back. Sealed with several coats of polyurethane, wood can be harmlessly damp-mopped—but puddles and heavy scrubbing eventually erode even this highly wear-resistant sealer.

Resilient floors— the strong, silent type

Resilient floors—both tile and sheet goods—take just about any kitchen mishap in stride. Water and spills can't penetrate them. They mop up easily, absorb kitchen clatter, and come in a wide spectrum of colors, patterns, and textures.

The most resilient of them all, cushioned vinyl, offers a sound-muffling ability that makes it popular with active families. Cushioned floors combine the durability and cleanability of vinyl with the comfort of carpeting.

Vinyl asbestos tiles are another good choice for the kitchen. They're durable and stain-resistant, and many come with a self-stick backing that makes them a favorite with do-it-yourselfers.

Solid vinyl tile is high-priced, but it wears very well, is available in beautifully clear colors, and has a luxurious appearance. The floor shown *opposite, upper right* demonstrates the design versatility of vinyl, and other tiles as well. Solid brown and white tiles alternate in a diagonal pattern, adding dynamism to a contemporary kitchen.

Forget about using asphalt tile in a kitchen; it has low resilience and poor resistance to grease and stains.

One last entry in this extensive category is seamless poured flooring. You can apply a poured floor over just about any material, including wood, concrete, and linoleum. First a liquid is spread out over the old surface, then vinyl chips are rolled in. After the liquid dries, this flooring is impervious to stains, moisture, and abrasion. Installation of a poured floor can be tricky, however; consider hiring a professional to do the work.

Carpeting magic

Like other flooring materials, kitchen carpeting has both strengths and weaknesses: it's comfortable to walk on, and a great sound absorber, but it tends to hold grease and food stains, and lets static electricity build up. You needn't worry about durability, though. Kitchen carpet holds up well underfoot—and under scrubbing. Top grades of polypropylene olefin are the easiest to clean and wear the best of all.

Hard-surface floors

Ceramic, slate and quarry tiles, brick, and other hard-surface floorings offer some of the most visually versatile surfaces available. You can choose from a rainbow of colors and a multitude of shapes to create a one-of-a-kind floor, such as the ruglike ceramic design shown *opposite, upper left.*

Since it isn't resilient, hard-surface flooring offers little comfort for tired feet—and if you drop a plate or glass, it'll almost certainly shatter to smithereens. On the other hand, a hard-surface floor is extremely tough and long-lasting—and a breeze to maintain.

Most installations are best done by professionals, but some types, such as mosaics mounted on sheets of mesh, are good candidates for do-it-yourself projects. Whether it's done by a pro or an amateur, hard-surface flooring installation requires considerable time and patience.

(continued)

YOUR FLOORING OPTIONS

	TYPES	EFFECTS
WOOD	**Strips (2¼ inches wide)** **Planks (random widths)** **Parquet tiles (1x1 foot)**	Strip flooring is commonly available in oak and maple; planks in oak and pine; parquet tiles often feature teak, walnut, and other exotic species. Some planks and tiles come prefinished; others—and strip flooring—can be stained any hue and sealed for any sheen from matte to high gloss. For design distinction, you can lay strips in herringbone, basket-weave, and other patterns.
RESILIENT FLOORING	**Vinyl asbestos tiles** **Solid vinyl tiles** **Sheet vinyl** **Cushioned sheet vinyl** **Poured vinyl**	You'll find a range of colors and textures, with patterns that range from abstract to simulations of brick, tile, and wood. Don't, however, expect to find a broad choice of clear, strong colors in resilient flooring. Most (except vinyl tiles) feature muted, variegated tones; clear colors are much more expensive to produce, and show scuffs more readily. Consider, too, whether you prefer a smooth or textured surface. Smooth tiles and sheet goods mop up easily, but show dirt and abrasion more readily.
CARPETING	**Nylon** **Polypropylene**	Carpeting comes in solid colors, plaids, stripes, geometric designs, and floral patterns. Multicolored patterns or tweeds show soil less than solid colors. Nylon is resilient underfoot, but absorbs water slightly; olefin isn't as resilient, but repels water. Both are available in standard-width rolls.
HARD-SURFACE FLOORING	**Ceramic tile** **Quarry tile** **Slate** **Brick** **Marble** **Terrazzo**	Design possibilities are virtually unlimited. Ceramic tile, the most popular hard-surface floor, has a glazed surface and a very wide color range; quarry tiles are baked clay, usually unglazed, and come in natural earth tones; characteristically dark gray, slate may be smooth or textured, regular or irregular in shape; marble is smooth, elegant, cool, and expensive; terrazzo is a man-made product consisting of marble or stone chips set in cement, then polished to a smooth, shiny, multicolored finish.

DURABILITY	USES	INSTALLATION	COST
Wood flooring holds up well, but requires frequent care. Dry-mop or vacuum daily, and remove stains with a cloth moistened in cleaner or wax. Unsealed floors should be protected with a hard, paste-type wax.	Wood makes special sense for an open-plan kitchen that you want to merge with adjacent areas. Planks complement a colonial or antique decorating scheme; parquet is ideal for more formal, traditional settings.	Strip and most plank floorings are best laid over a surface in good condition. Some planks lend themselves to do-it-yourself installation, as do wood tiles. Some tiles are available with self-stick backing.	Unfinished oak strips are the least expensive; other types range from moderate to costly, depending upon grade, species, and whether or not the wood has been prefinished. For all, keep installation costs in mind.
No-wax surfaces require the least care—simply damp-mop with mild detergent; others require waxing after cleaning. High-grade cushioned sheet vinyl is the most durable; others are vulnerable to dents from pointed items such as chair legs, and require more frequent care.	Resilient flooring is far and away the preferred material in new homes and remodeled kitchens. Because it's almost impervious to grease, tar, sand, and other dirt that travels by foot, you might decide that resilient flooring is a must for a kitchen with direct access to the outdoors.	Tiles are classics for do-it-yourselfers; some even come with a self-stick backing that eliminates any need for a separate adhesive. Cushioned sheet vinyl, which is loose-laid without adhesive, also lends itself to homeowner installations. Other sheet goods and poured flooring are best installed by professionals.	Vinyl asbestos tiles are the least expensive. Sheet goods vary widely in price, depending mainly on face grade and pattern. Solid sheet vinyl and vinyl tiles are moderately expensive. If your subfloor is uneven, you may have to put down an underlayment first, at added cost.
Carpet wears well, but spills require immediate action to avoid permanent stains. For general maintenance you need a powdered dry cleaner or aerosol foaming spray and a vacuum. One way to check a carpet's durability is to bend back a corner and see how much of the backing shows; the more backing you see, the less fiber you're getting.	Cushy and highly sound-absorbent, kitchen carpeting is appreciated by cooks who are on their feet a lot, and in big kitchens where clatter is a problem. However, if your household includes small children or pets—or if you're a messy cook—you may decide to opt for a flooring material that's easier to spot-clean.	Roll goods are best installed by professionals, who may glue carpeting in place or secure it with tack strips. Carpeting lays easily over any existing surface except cushioned sheet vinyl.	Moderate to moderately low compared to natural materials and hard surfaces. Price depends on density, face material, and pattern.
Hard-surface floors, exceptionally durable, need only occasional damp-mopping. Some quarry tiles are porous and require a stain-resistant sealer; wax slate, brick, and marble periodically. Grout joints may need occasional scouring and treatment with a mildew retardant.	For sheer beauty and permanence, it's hard to top the appearance of a hard-surface floor. And because most hard-surface materials work as well outdoors as they do in, you might choose them for a kitchen that flows outside to an adjacent patio.	You might attempt installing a ceramic, slate, or quarry tile floor yourself, but all of the others are strictly for pros; cutting and grouting are tricky operations. Also, hard-surface materials must be laid over a sub-surface that's dead level and smooth.	Ceramic, slate, quarry tile, and brick are moderate to expensive; terrazzo and especially marble, very expensive. Add the cost involved in providing a proper sub-surface, and you'll probably find that hard-surface flooring is the most expensive way to go.

COUNTERS

Counter tops run a close second to floors in the amount of punishment they have to stand up to. What with chopping and pounding, heat and cold, stains, moisture, and three-times-a-day cleaning —counters are really a kitchen's workbenches. If yours are beginning to show their age, take heart; renewing kitchen counters is easier than you might think.

At first glance, face-lifting counter tops looks like an imposing job. Can you lay new materials over the old? If not, how are you going to remove the existing surface? And how the devil are you going to get a tight seal around the sink, range, and any other flush-mounted item?

Open up a base cabinet, study the underside of your counters, and you'll discover that you needn't worry about any of these problems. Counter tops merely *look* like they're a permanent part of the cabinets that support them. Actually, they're secured by screws driven up from underneath. This means you simply remove the sink and those screws, slide out the old top, and slip a new one in its place. The switch can be made in a single day.

Whether you build your own counters, have them custom-built, or order stock replacements, measurements are critical. So are the materials you select. Here are the three major ways to go. Once again, a chart on the two pages that follow compares these surface options in greater detail.

Plastic, plastic, plastic
Durable, colorful, and easy-to-clean, plastic is the most widely used counter surfacing. Plastic falls into three general categories: laminate, vinyl, and solid acrylic.

Laminate—often called Formica, a popular trade name —consists of sheets of $1/16$-inch-thick material bonded to ¾-inch plywood or particleboard. Laminated tops may be "self-edged" with a separate strip that gives a 90-degree corner at the front edge, or "post-formed" for a rolled edge like the one shown *opposite, center left*.

Laminated plastic counters resist moisture, grease, stains, soaps and detergents, hot water, and moderate heat. Don't set a hot pan or iron on laminate, though; your counter top will blister. You have to be careful with sharp knives, too. Laminate nicks fairly easily, and scratches quickly collect dirt and grease.

Vinyl counter tops are similar to laminate, but more resilient. Again, be careful with sharp knives and hot pans. Keep hot water off vinyl, too; it can stretch and buckle the surface.

Solid acrylic tops are plastic all the way through their ¾-inch thickness, and often look like marble. They're also vulnerable to scratches and high heat, and weigh considerably more than either laminate or vinyl tops.

Wood takes a beating
For slicing, chopping, and pounding, hardwood counter tops or counter inserts are the gourmet cook's favorite. Left alone, small scratches and nicks add character, or you can smooth them out with sandpaper or steel wool.

Butcher block, the most common wood counter, consists of 1½-inch-thick strips of maple glued edge to edge to achieve a smooth, continuous surface. Because it's thicker than standard tops, a butcher-block replacement counter top will raise your counter surface, and plumbing connections may need to be modified.

Another way to achieve a wood counter top is to build one with oak or maple tongue-and-groove flooring glued and nailed to a plywood base. The counter and backsplash shown *opposite, above* were made from red oak and sealed with four coats of polyurethane.

Wood counter tops don't like water, so don't let spills stand on them. You can't set hot pans on wood, either; they'll scorch the surface.

The hard choice: hard-surface counters
This category includes a potpourri of different materials —tile, granite, ceramic glass, stainless steel, and natural and synthetic marble. Tile makes a good-looking, heat- and scratch-proof surface like the one pictured *opposite, center right*. Tile counters are easy to keep clean, though grout joints may need occasional attention.

Ceramic glass—the same material used for smooth-top ranges—works best as an insert that's impervious to high heat or scratches. It's easy to clean, and it resists most spots and stains.

Stainless steel, widely used in restaurant kitchens, isn't fazed by high heat, grease, or moisture. It's prone to water spots, though, and to light surface scratches.

Natural marble is cool, smooth, and a favorite of bakers and candy makers. It's predictably heavy and costly, though, and stains easily. Synthetic marble like the handsome white tops shown *opposite, below* is less porous than natural, and is less affected by stains and grease.

(continued)

COUNTERS
(continued)

YOUR COUNTER OPTIONS

	TYPES	EFFECTS
PLASTIC	**Self-edged laminate** **Post-formed laminate** **Vinyl** **Solid acrylic**	No longer do you have to settle for the mottled, speckled, or star-burst patterns of early-day plastic counter tops. Laminates now come in a wide range of clear colors (including pure white), highly convincing wood and marble look-alike motifs, and patterns aplenty. Surfaces vary, too, from slick and shiny to matte and leatherlike. Vinyls include a smaller but still impressive range of choices. Most solid acrylic tops replicate marble, but some other patterns and clear colors are also available. Whatever look you want to achieve with new counters, you can do it with plastic. Be advised, though, that few materials dealers could possibly stock a complete selection; you probably will need to special-order less popular colors or designs.
WOOD	**Butcher block** **Flooring**	Butcher block looks exactly like what it is—a warm, solid, and rugged work surface that harmonizes with all but the most formal of decors. You have to settle for butcher block's natural maple coloring, though; it can't readily be stained to create other tones. Flooring offers more versatility. You can mix or match wood grains, lay boards in patterns, or bleach or stain them to different hues. And wood ages with dignity. Years of use and proper care give it a handsome, mellow patina.
HARD-SURFACE MATERIALS	**Tile** **Ceramic glass** **Stainless steel** **Natural marble** **Synthetic marble**	Tile offers an almost limitless range of colors, shapes, and glazes, though matte finishes provide greater resistance to scratching; some tiles, such as quarry and slate, are porous and should be protected with sealer. Ceramic glass, which can't be cut, comes in standard sizes and several color choices. Stainless steel can be rolled over edges and up backsplashes for a smooth, sleek unbroken surface. With natural marble, color choices are determined by availability and are directly proportional to cost. Synthetics, sometimes known as cultured marble, are made by embedding finely ground marble chips in plastic; the result has the color and veining of the real thing. Hard-surface counters are noisier than others, and are unforgiving in contact with china and glassware.

DURABILITY	USES	INSTALLATION	COST
Plastic resists grease and stains, and cleans easily with soap and water or a mild abrasive. Don't subject it to high heat or sharp knives. Beware, too, of hard blows; they can chip plastic, especially at edges. Plastic tops hold up well over the years, though ultimately they begin to dull and wear thin.	Ideal for all kitchen counter areas except those adjacent to ranges and ovens. Here, consider a hard-surface insert that can serve as a landing pad for hot cookware. For chopping you might want a second hardwood insert—or a separate chopping block kept conveniently at hand.	You can order post-formed tops by the running foot, with a sink cutout where you need it. Some self-edged counters come this way, too, or you can have them made to your specifications. Laminating plastic is only a moderately tricky do-it-yourself job; installing tops is fairly easy, provided you've measured carefully. Acrylic tops are surprisingly heavy; cabinets underneath may need beefing up.	Laminate counter tops range all the way from inexpensive to moderately costly, depending mainly upon the color and pattern you want. Vinyl costs a bit more than most laminates; solid acrylic tops are the most expensive of all.
With occasional maintenance, wood lasts a lifetime. Butcher block should be rubbed down periodically with mineral oil to reseal the grain and prevent splitting; flooring needs a fresh coat of polyurethane every few years. Both can be completely sanded down and refinished if they become badly scarred. Their main drawback: neither of them is highly resistant to heat or moisture.	Wood excels as inserts or for entire runs of counter. Remember that you needn't stick exclusively to a single counter material throughout your kitchen. You might, for instance, decide to use wood on a center island where chopping and other prep jobs take place, laminate at the sink area, and a hard-surface material near the range and oven.	Suppliers of butcher block sell their product by the running foot, sometimes complete with an integral backsplash, and will usually make a sink cutout where you need it; installing butcher block is an only moderately difficult two-person job. Assembling a top from flooring calls for lots of cutting, fitting, and sanding.	Butcher block is relatively expensive. Flooring is moderately costly provided you build the counter yourself. Buy only top-grade lumber, though, and order 15 to 20 percent more than you need; cracks in a counter trap dirt, so you'll want to reject any boards that are even slightly warped.
All last indefinitely, and most are very easy to maintain. Tile grouting gradually discolors and requires cleaning; stubborn spots on ceramic glass can be removed with a cleaner sold for smooth-top ranges; wipe water spots off stainless steel with a soft, dry cloth, and take care that you don't scratch it; natural marble is porous, prone to stains, and difficult to keep clean; synthetic marble is nonporous and much easier to maintain than natural marble.	High cost and other limitations make most hard-surface materials better suited for use as inserts or in limited areas, but if you want a truly luxurious kitchen, go ahead and treat yourself to tile, stainless steel, or marble counter tops. Tile and marble are appropriate with almost any kitchen style; stainless steel gives a sleek, industrial look.	Only tile lends itself to do-it-yourself installation; replace existing counters with ¾-inch exterior-grade plywood, then lay tiles atop this base. You can order stainless steel tops from a restaurant supply house; these can be made up with integral sinks for a one-piece molded effect. Marble —both natural and synthetic —may need special structural support. Installation is tricky, even for pros.	Tile is moderate to moderately high in cost, especially if you select an imported tile, which is subject to duties. Glass and synthetic marble are both moderate, but installation costs for marble push up its bill. Stainless steel, sold by the running foot, is expensive. With natural marble, the sky's the limit.

RESTYLING CABINETS

As you've seen on the preceding pages, walls and ceilings, floors, and counters all lend themselves to face-lifting with fairly standard materials and techniques. But what, short of replacing them, can you do about worn, dated-looking cabinets? The answer: leave their innards alone, but put on fresh fronts.

At first glance, the photographs *opposite* seem to picture four different kitchens. Compare them more closely, however, and you'll discover you're looking at the same room (a studio set, actually) that we've styled, restyled, restyled, and restyled again. The project demonstrates just how varied cabinet cosmetology can be.

Four for-instances

At *upper left,* new smoked-glass doors front the wall cabinets. We cut the arched openings from ¾-inch birch plywood and attached ¼-inch smoked glass to the doors' backs with L-shaped mirror brackets. (You may need to cut back cabinet shelves to make room for the glass.) All the trim and lower cabinets were then laminated with ⅛-inch birch plywood. Natural-tone tile harmonizes with the wood.

Paint plays Pygmalion for the cabinets shown at *upper right.* First everything was treated to a fresh coat of white, then graphic accent strips were applied. Red plastic laminate on the counter brings out the red stripe above and below. This treatment works especially well on flat wood or metal slab doors.

In the version at *lower left,* we did away with the wall cabinets' doors entirely, and replaced them with pull-down canvas shades. We made the shades with lightweight canvas cut 8 inches longer and ¼ inch narrower than the openings, ran ¾-inch dowels through the shade bottoms,

and cut out handholds. More dowels—these 1 inch in diameter and 4 inches long—serve as new pulls on the base cabinets and drawers. Each dowel was slightly flattened along the back side and attached with screws driven from inside the doors and drawers. Colorful ceramic tile brightens this otherwise-neutral scheme.

Knotty pine puts a fresh face on the cabinets shown at *lower right.* We built the doors of ¾-inch boards beveled on the front vertical edges to form V grooves; you could achieve a similar effect with tongue-and-groove pine paneling. Those hefty pulls began life as handles for masons' finishing trowels.

By now you're probably beginning to get the idea about cabinet restyling possibilities—that they're limited only by the energy you're willing to put into doing the work. Most cabinet redos fall into one or a combination of three main categories. Let's look at them briefly here, and in greater detail on pages 58 and 59.

Spruce up surfaces

Superficial changes give cabinets an entirely new life. Treat them to a new paint job. Cover doors and/or end panels with scrubbable wall covering. Strip down to bare wood, stain, and seal with polyurethane. Apply plastic laminate and your surfaces will remain bright and clean for years.

All these treatments take time—painting cabinets, for example, is a tedious chore—but require only minimal outlays for materials. And because you'll see the difference right away, you'll be inspired to push on with the job.

Of course, there's no point in redressing doors that don't fit, so make sure yours don't suffer from bows, cracks, or warps. If they're in poor or dubious condition, you might be better off to simply replace them, as explained *below.*

Apply new trimmings

Details can make a surprising difference, too. Tired of blank, featureless doors and drawer fronts? Consider perking them up with moldings. These make special sense on ultra-utilitarian-looking metal cabinets.

Or perhaps you'd like to do something about old, tarnished knobs and pulls. Again, no problem; hardware and specialty stores stock an astonishing variety of replacements.

Change doors

There's nothing sacred about the existing doors on your cabinets, either. Most cabinet dimensions are standardized, which means you can probably find ready-made replacement doors at a cabinet dealer. Of course, you also can build your own new doors, as we did—or simply leave the doors off, paint cabinet interiors a lively color, and show off your kitchen gear on open shelving.

One last suggestion: if you're not at all satisfied with your present cabinets, consider replacing the whole lot of them with new units. Pages 96 and 97 tell what you need to know about shopping for kitchen cabinets.

(continued)

RESTYLING CABINETS
(continued)

YOUR CABINET RESTYLING OPTIONS

	OPTIONS	EFFECTS
SPRUCE UP SURFACES	**Paint** **Wall coverings** **Stain** **Plastic laminate**	Paint offers a multitude of possibilities, ranging from simple, solid colors to two-tones, stripes, outlining, and antiquing. Consider only gloss or semigloss finishes; flat finishes won't hold up. Wall coverings can cover entire cabinet surfaces or serve as insert panels surrounded by paint; choose one of the durable vinyl types discussed on pages 46 and 47. Stain makes sense only if your cabinets have a handsome wood-grain (test in a limited area before you commit to a major stripping job); also consider staining only doors and drawer fronts, finishing cabinet rails, stiles, and end panels with paint. With laminate, thinner $\frac{1}{32}$-inch-thick material is suitable for vertical surfaces; for economy you might want to laminate doors, drawer fronts, rails, and stiles, but treat interiors and end panels with paint. More about laminate on pages 52-55.
APPLY NEW TRIMMINGS	**Moldings** **Pulls and knobs** **Hinges**	Wood or plastic moldings—sometimes sold in kit form—can create almost any design motif; you can select anything from flat screen molding to ornate "carvings." Moldings also offer a good way to frame a wall covering insert, separate two paint colors, or trim the edges of laminate. Pulls, knobs, and hinges express a kitchen's character; sleek hardware says contemporary, wrought iron harks back to colonial times, and so on. The range of manufactured hardware styles is mind-boggling, and you can also make your own knobs and pulls out of almost anything the hand can grasp.
CHANGE DOORS	**Stock** **Custom** **Open shelves**	Stock doors, often available from cabinet dealers, fit standard openings and come in a variety of styles, from flush to panel. Custom-built doors offer a wider range of designs, including glass inserts and recessed panels; make these yourself or order them from a cabinet shop. Removing doors opens up cabinet interiors for a whole new range of design possibilities. Adding new doors or removing old ones has high impact on kitchen decor, often giving the look of all-new cabinets.

DURABILITY	USES	INSTALLATION	COST
Glossy surfaces wipe down easily with mild detergent and water. Paint can chip, requiring touch-up. Scrubbable vinyl wall coverings stand up to repeated washings; don't use ordinary, untreated papers here. Stained surfaces need two coats of polyurethane to aid cleanability. Plastic is the most durable/cleanable of all.	You can renew almost all cabinet surfaces with one or a combination of these materials —and give your kitchen a fresh personality, as well. Which you choose depends on the condition of your cabinets, the look you want, and the money and effort you're willing to invest in achieving it.	The success of a good paint job depends largely upon the prep work; wash down well, sand, and spot-prime imperfections. Steel cabinets should be sprayed; consider taking doors and drawers to an automotive paint shop. Wall coverings, especially self-adhesive types, make quick cover-ups. Staining is easy, but stripping off old paint or varnish is a tedious, messy chore. Applying plastic laminate is a bit tricky; you might want to hire a professional.	Painting is low to moderate in cost if you do the work yourself, moderate to high if you hire it done. Wall coverings can range from low to moderately high, depending on the grade and design you select. Staining is low in materials costs, high on elbow grease. Plastic laminate runs moderate to high, depending on who does the work.
Select moldings with an eye toward cleanability; the more decoration you add to cabinets, the more scrubbing you'll have to do. Trim also should be well sealed with paint or polyurethane. Hardware "bargains" cost more in the long run, and saddle you with the daily nuisance of loose screws, missing pulls, and sloppy hinges; invest in quality door and drawer hardware from the outset.	Moldings can give a completely new look to cabinets; combine them with paint, wall coverings, or stain to add interest to ordinary flush doors and drawers. Quality knobs, pulls, and hinges reward you with smooth operation and durable good looks.	Cut moldings with a fine-tooth saw. Glue lighter trim in place; use glue and a few brads with others. Hinges can be tricky to install; pulls and knobs are easy, but you'll probably have to fill or cover up holes left by the old hardware.	Most moldings are inexpensive. Quality hardware can run surprisingly high; individual items don't seem costly, but a typical kitchen has quite a few pulls, knobs, and hinges; pulls and knobs are easy to upgrade later on.
Polyurethane or factory-applied coatings are fairly durable and wipe down easily. Plastic laminate is better yet. Open shelves are notorious dirt-catchers; periodically you have to wash all your dishes and cookware, as well as the shelves themselves. For this reason, you might decide on open shelving only for frequently used items.	If your existing doors are badly deteriorated, get rid of them and use open shelves, or replace them with new ones. Tight-fitting, smooth-swinging doors are a joy to open and close—the next best thing to a brand-new kitchen.	If your cabinets are standard sizes, stock doors will fit easily, but you can bet their hinges won't match up with your old ones. Hanging cabinet doors is a moderately tricky do-it-yourself job. Removing doors is easy, of course, but then you have to fill and cover holes left by hinges, catches, and other hardware.	New doors are normally the most expensive face-lifting option, but also the most effective. Making them yourself can greatly cut costs; realize, though, that your effort will be multiplied by the number of openings you have to deal with. "Doors" on open shelves are virtually free, if you don't mind the extra dusting and cleaning that open shelves entail.

COORDINATING WALLS, FLOORS, COUNTERS, AND CABINETS

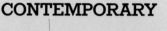

COUNTRY

CONTEMPORARY

Country is a lighthearted look, simple and comfortable, informal and charming. To capture the essence of this cheery style, strive for a kitchen that might have been transplanted from the farmhouses of a generation ago.

Country calls for light and sunny treatment. Blue gives instant atmosphere, especially if you combine it with white or yellow. Beams added to walls or ceilings reinforce the rustic look, as do wide boards used as a dado above weathered wood paneling. Texture paint applied to "beamed" walls adds even more character.

If you're looking for wall covering, you can't go wrong with blue and white checks and other homey patterns.

You want a rugged, earthy floor in a country kitchen. Brick is ideal —either the real thing or a patterned vinyl. Floors of quarry tile and wood planking also give a natural, country aura.

Counters can be butcher block, ceramic tile in a primitive pattern, or solid-color plastic laminate that blends with other kitchen colors.

Cabinets should have the warm glow of mellow wood. Stenciled and painted designs are also very much at home here. Complement them with simple brass hardware. For more about country kitchens, see pages 24-27.

Contemporary strips away anything that's unnecessary, uses strong colors, and puts the emphasis on function and efficiency.

This means there's no room for busy patterns. Make walls solid expanses of color, or pure chalky white if you have strong colors elsewhere. Considering a wall covering? Opt for a tailored, textured vinyl, a shimmering metallic foil, or an upbeat geometric print.

Other materials that seem automatically contemporary are chrome, glass, stainless steel, and plastic.

Select a floor covering that makes a good, plain background—vinyl works well here, as does carpeting, and natural woods such as strip oak or maple.

Counter tops, too, should be simple and sleek. Good choices are solid-color plastic laminate, butcher block, and stainless steel. And the same material selection goes for cabinets; install plain, unpaneled doors of handsomely grained wood, simple metal fronts, or plastic laminates.

For knobs and pulls, clean-lined metal hardware—with brushed or polished chrome finishes —augments a contemporary mood; sparely shaped wood or ceramic designs work well here, too.

To learn more about the clean, nearly Spartan beauty of contemporary styling, see pages 30 and 31.

COLONIAL

Colonial has been a favorite kitchen style for generations now, and it's easy to see why. Warm and mellow, and elegantly simple, it expresses the spirit of Yankee pride and practicality.

In a colonial kitchen, paint the walls white, either textured or smooth. Or you can select from a wide array of Early American wall coverings in small prints, checks, or documentary designs. For real colonial atmosphere, combine paper with a dado or chair rail applied to the wall.

Wood flooring is a natural, whether you lay down genuine planks or install resilient flooring in a wood pattern. A brick surface is another good choice. To gain further authenticity, top

whatever floor covering you choose with a braided or rag rug.

For counter tops, consider butcher block or plastic laminate in a wood-grain pattern. A natural wood look is a good choice for cabinets, too, as are doors and drawer fronts that look as if they were made from white-painted planks. Hammered wrought-iron hinges and other hardware create a colonial feeling almost instantly.

Pages 36 and 37 tell more about colonial styling; Chapter 2 also presents a variety of other looks you can achieve with a kitchen face-lift.

TRADITIONAL

Dark woods, paneled doors, elegant hardware, and somber colors characterize traditional motifs. The trick with traditional is to blend all these elements into a kitchen that looks formal but not gloomy.

Paint walls in pastels or muted tones, cover them with vinyl in a classic wallpaper pattern, or put up rich wood or wood-look paneling. With care, you also can combine a couple of these materials—paneled wainscotting, for instance, with paint or a "paper" wall covering above.

For the floor, you might choose ceramic tile in a geometric pattern, wood parquet, or a resilient covering that resembles materials used centuries ago.

Here again, stay away from any surface that's bright and shiny.

Marble—either natural or synthetic—is ideal for traditional counters, but you can achieve the same effect with plastic laminate or tile. But avoid butcher block; it's a bit too informal for this kitchen style.

Elegant wood cabinets are a must in a traditional kitchen. If yours are on the plain side, embellish them with moldings and shiny or antique brass knobs and pulls.

For more about creating a traditional look in your kitchen, turn to pages 40 and 41.

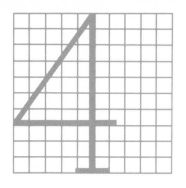

GETTING A
NEW KITCHEN
ON PAPER

If your kitchen seems hopelessly out of date, you may have thought about a complete, to-the-studs remodeling. Trouble is, most of us find it difficult to visualize all the possibilities for what amounts to the most complex room in any house. The key: break down your planning process into a series of steps that you follow in a particular sequence—and give yourself plenty of opportunity to change your mind. This chapter takes you step by step through that all-important planning stage, and introduces you to a versatile system that lets you try out your ideas—all of them —at the kitchen table.

PLANNING WITH CUTOUTS AND GRAPH PAPER

A successful kitchen remodeling starts with a clear picture of the space you have available. Forget for the moment about existing cabinets, counters, appliances, and other components. What you want at this point is a floor-plan view of an empty room—your kitchen on a clean slate.

Your plan can be simple but it has to be accurate, and that means taking careful measurements. Inch by inch, every dimension contributes to a win or lose situation.

To avoid errors, don't measure with a yardstick or a cloth tape. A yardstick is seldom accurate enough, and a cloth tape can sag and throw off your measurements. Use only a steel tape or a carpenter's folding rule.

First, a rough sketch
Start your planning project by making a rough floor-plan sketch of your kitchen. Indicate the positions of windows, doors, and any jogs or architectural details in the walls. Now you can start measuring.

Begin in one corner of the kitchen, measuring at countertop height (36 inches above the floor). Measure from the corner to the first interruption of the wall surface, such as a window or door. Record that measurement on your rough floor-plan sketch.

Next measure across the window or door from one outside edge of the frame to the other. Record that measurement. Continue in segments across the wall, recording each measurement separately.

When you've finished a wall, total the individual measurements. Then, as a double check, measure the entire wall from corner to corner. If there's any difference in the two figures, start over.

Now to graph paper
When you have all walls measured accurately, transfer these measurements to graph paper. Let each ¼-inch square represent 1 foot of kitchen wall space. Use a ruler to keep lines straight, and indicate exactly where windows and doors are located (use dotted lines to outline the entire area through which doors will swing). Also pinpoint locations of lights, gas connections, water lines, electrical connections, and heating or cooling outlets. (More about these essentials on pages 78 and 79.)

Build it on paper
With the walls, doors, and windows drawn up, it's time to move in your cabinets and appliances—all on paper, of course. To make this job easier, we've provided a section of templates in the back of the book (pages 154-156). Here you'll find basic cabinet and appliance shapes you can trace, cut out, and position.

In designing your kitchen, exercise creativity, by all means. But also keep in mind these standard dimensions.
• Factory-built base cabinets are made in 3-inch increments from 12 to 48 inches wide, and are 24 inches deep.
• Wall cabinets range from 12 to 48 inches wide and 12 to 13 inches deep.
• Appliances placed opposite one another require 5 to 6 feet of clearance so doors can open without interference.
• Counter surfaces are usually 36 inches high.
• Allow 15 to 18 inches of clearance between a counter and the undersides of overhanging wall cabinets for small appliances such as a blender, stand mixer, and coffee maker.
• For standard-depth cabinets over a sink, allow at least 30 inches above the sink rim.

Draw the outline of your kitchen on ¼-inch graph paper, indicating placement of windows and doors. Remember, one square of graph paper equals 1 foot of kitchen space.

After first covering a piece of tracing paper with yellow marker to improve its visibility on your floor plan, trace the shapes of cabinets and appliances, using the templates on pages 154-156.

Cut out the traced outlines of cabinets and appliances (with doors open to indicate space in use). Position kitchen "components" on the graph paper floor plan, rearranging them to design the kitchen that meets your needs.

GETTING A NEW KITCHEN ON PAPER

WHICH OF THESE SIX BASIC LAYOUTS WOULD WORK BEST FOR YOU?

Every kitchen has the same basic ingredients—cabinets, counter tops, and appliances. It's how you arrange these "givens" that makes the difference in the way your kitchen functions. Granted, some kitchen plans are dictated by the architecture of the space. That's where the six basic plans shown here come into play. But within these six kitchen designs, you still have the flexibility to create an area that will save you time and energy—or, in the absence of thought-through goals, to create a monster. It's up to you. How do you want your kitchen laid out?

The eternal triangle
You don't need a time-and-motion study of your kitchen habits to tell you that work centers comfortably close will save both time and energy. You'll also save extra steps if your work centers fit the logical sequence of food storage, preparation, cooking, serving, and cleanup.
• Create a *work triangle*. In all but a one-wall kitchen, it's possible to arrange the refrigerator, sink, and range to form a triangle—proven to be the most efficient layout for kitchen centers.
• If you want to cut out unnecessary hiking, the three sides of the work triangle should total between 12 and 22 feet.
• The distance between the sink and range should be 4 to 6 feet.
• The distance between the range and refrigerator should be 4 to 9 feet.
• The distance between the refrigerator and sink should be 4 to 7 feet.
Increasing the distances between the points of the triangle beyond these limits only adds needless kitchen mileage and

fatigue. On the other hand, cutting measurements short of these limits will cramp your kitchen to the point where it—and you—stop functioning efficiently.

U-shape
If you've got the space and the right room architecture, and you want a kitchen that's tops in efficiency, this is your layout. As you can see in the *upper left* drawing, *opposite*, the U-shape gives you three full walls of working kitchen. But don't attempt this arrangement unless you have at least 8 feet along both the length and the width of your room.
A U-shape plan offers a logical sequence of work centers with minimal distances between. As an alternative, the sink often goes at the end of the U, with the refrigerator and range on the two side walls. An extra dividend you get with any U-shape kitchen is the absence of through traffic in the work areas.

One-wall
The one-wall or pullman kitchen plan shown at *center left, opposite*, usually makes most sense in spaces where width is limited. Though this layout precludes the step-saving triangular arrangement of work centers, it still can be efficient, particularly if the sink is between the range and the refrigerator. The only liability of the

one-wall kitchen relates to its architecture: because it usually has a door at each end, through traffic can be an annoying interruption.

L-shape
With two adjacent walls used for work centers, an L-shape layout forms a natural triangle and is protected from traffic through the rest of the area. This kitchen plan, shown at *bottom left, opposite*, permits flexibility in the arrangement of appliances, storage, and counters; the work itself, however, should flow from refrigerator to sink to cooking and serving areas. Get too eccentric in appliance placement and you may be building in a lot of backtracking and reduced efficiency.
If designed with care, this kitchen layout accommodates two cooks expeditiously.

Galley
The galley or corridor plan, shown at *top right, opposite*, places appliances and cabinets along opposite walls. This arrangement best promotes efficient work habits when the sink and refrigerator are on one wall and the range on the opposite wall. If counters are reasonably close, the triangular work pattern can be compact and efficient. In a particularly large space, you might want to

reduce the distance between work centers with an island.
Watch for traffic in a galley kitchen. Often a door at each end brackets this space, causing more walk-through traffic than you want.

Island
An island in a kitchen can shorten the distance between sink, range, and refrigerator—see the drawing at *center right, opposite*. An island arrangement works particularly well in the cavernous kitchens of older homes, adding both visual interest to the expanse of open space and efficiency to the flow of work.
Some kitchen planners choose to install the range or cooktop in the island; others use this freestanding unit for the sink and dishwasher in a cleanup center. Either way, plan an island large enough for counter space on both sides of the sink or range.

Peninsula
When you've run out of wall space, but still have floor space available, a peninsula can increase your kitchen's workability. As shown at *bottom right, opposite*, a peninsula extends into open floor space, perpendicular to the cabinet units of a wall: use it to house your range or sink.
By planning the proper size and position of a kitchen peninsula, you can create a work triangle that's highly efficient, and assign wall space to cabinets for increased storage.

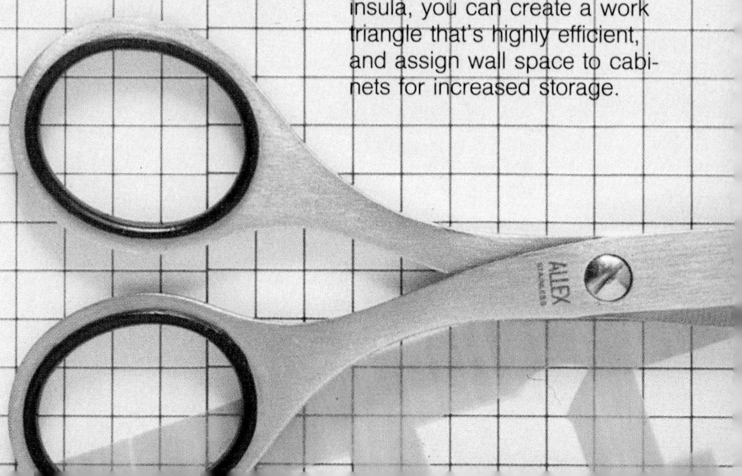

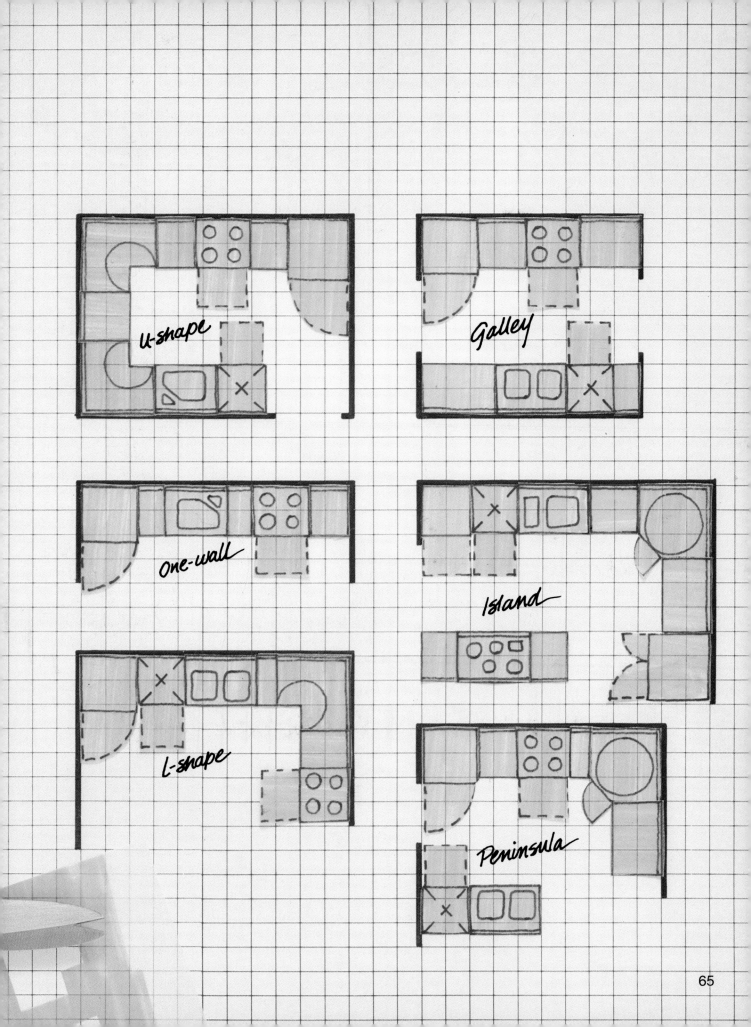

U-shape

Galley

One-wall

Island

L-shape

Peninsula

65

CAN YOU EXPAND INTO ADJACENT SPACE?

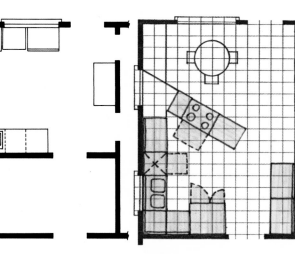

BEFORE   **AFTER**

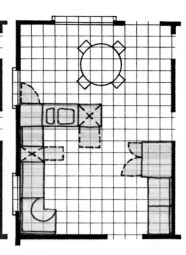

ALTERNATE

When you're suffering from kitchen cramps, the most logical place to look for relief is to the walls that constrict the area. What's on the other side of them? And is nearby space, the way it currently functions, really essential to your lifestyle? You might find that an old pantry, breakfast nook, utility room, or enclosed porch could provide just the extra square feet you need to give your kitchen breathing room.

Look first to the rooms adjacent to your kitchen. They're where it's easiest to gain the added space you want. But remember, kitchen expansion is a give-and-take proposition. Chances are, the area you're eyeing is not sitting there totally unused; it's already performing some function of its own. Here's the trade-off: in order to acquire that room's space, you may have to factor its function into your remodeled kitchen. In the case of a breakfast nook or dining area, that's no sacrifice. If the adjacent area is a utility room, mud room, or laundry, you may have a greater challenge relocating the coveted space's function.

Before you tear down walls
Let's now assume adjacent space is available. How do you assimilate it into your kitchen? In most cases, you don't. You treat the combined spaces as an entirely new area, which gives you the opportunity to completely rearrange your kitchen, to add more storage, more features, even more appliances.

With that kind of fresh-start approach to kitchen remodel-

ing, you'll need to sit down and list all the things you want your kitchen to have and do. And list them in order of their importance to you.

Once you've enumerated all the elements you want in your kitchen, it's time to come to grips with one of the toughest factors in any remodeling —space allocation. Although you've added more square footage in the annexation, you won't know if your dream kitchen will fit until you've worked out the details on graph paper.

The pencil-and-paper stage
Using our guidelines on pages 62 and 63, measure your kitchen and draw it to scale on graph paper, noting all critical dimensions. Next, measure the adjacent room and draw it on the graph-paper layout in relationship to the kitchen. Be sure to indicate all windows, doors, plumbing, electrical outlets, and heat outlets. Now, eliminate the wall that separates the two areas. (To keep your measurements accurate, you'll also need to measure and represent on the layout the thickness of the wall you're thinking of removing.)

One of the hardest obstacles to overcome in looking at the newly formed space is a tendency to think of your kitchen as it exists now. Unless you intend to retain the core of your kitchen and simply expand storage or eating spaces, forget about your present kitchen. Start over with basic appliance and cabinet templates and work through several different kitchen layouts—there's never just one way to design a room.

Try some new angles
The family whose kitchen is shown here found that an interesting angled peninsula gave them a cook center that would overlook the dining area, planning center, and patio (also see the photograph, *opposite*). Our plan, *above center,* shows how this imaginative kitchen fits into space that was previously both kitchen and breakfast nook.

Still another possibility for this kitchen is shown in the alternate plan, *above right.* Here a right-angle peninsula becomes the sink/dishwasher cleanup center, incorporating cabinet space that's accessible from the eating area and the planning center.

SHOULD YOU CONSIDER AN ADDITION?

You've exhausted all possibilities of gaining more kitchen space by acquisition. There are no adjacent rooms to produce the space you need. There are no more clever ways to double up on functions or storage or family meal times. And there's no fairy godmother to wave a magic wand and make your kitchen as spacious or as convenient as you'd like. At this point you have only one recourse—short of moving—and that's to add on.

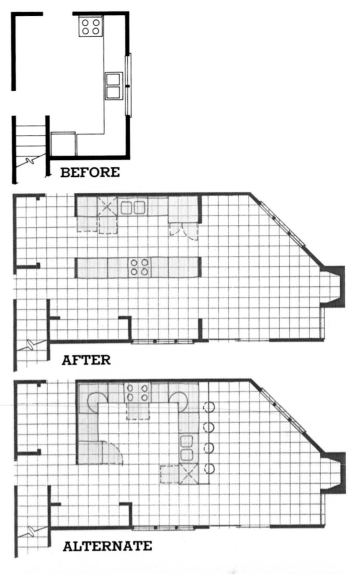

BEFORE

AFTER

ALTERNATE

Most families don't consider an addition until their kitchen is on the critical list and there are no other cures available. But most families who do add on find they usually gain more than just the kitchen they've always wanted. The new kitchen often comes hand in hand with a family room, with larger and more conveniently located dining space, or with any one of several architectural improvements that can make a home more livable.

Add up before you add on
When an addition begins to evolve from a dream to a strong possibility, it's time to think through what you want the new space to do. Consider (1) how much space you can afford to add on; (2) the lot space on which you can expand; (3) the functions you want the addition to perform; (4) whether you should simply move out the exterior kitchen wall, or involve other areas of the house as well; (5) whether your kitchen will stay where it is and expand, or move to another area of the house; and most important (6), what you want your kitchen to do that it couldn't do before?

What about the kitchen?
No one knows your kitchen better than you do. You're the expert when it comes to analyzing its strong points and its flaws. List both. What features of your present kitchen would you like to retain? What about it could be improved? And what will you be happiest not having to live with anymore? These are the questions to keep in mind when you develop your new kitchen plan.

But don't limit your planning to the kitchen exclusively. When you have a scale drawing of the area to be added on, play with some plans on paper. For instance, add the dining table and indicate the furnishings you'll want in the family room portion. When you've earmarked so much space per function, you can settle down to the serious business of laying out your kitchen with just the right arrangement of work centers and storage.

Try several arrangements
The kitchen/family room addition shown here was created by bumping out the old kitchen wall. In the new open area, a kitchen was installed that differed wholly from the original. This one, seen in the after plan, *right,* is a galley kitchen with one of the walls serving more as an island than as an enclosing structure. The long cooking counter, *opposite,* is open above the counter top to retain the area's spacious feeling. And the arrangement of this kitchen center also creates a natural corridor that lets traffic move to the family room, shown *below right,* without interrupting activities in the kitchen's work areas.

A second arrangement, our alternate at *bottom right,* has a peninsula that divides the kitchen and family room and also creates a very workable U-shaped plan for the kitchen itself. Here, the sink/dishwasher cleanup center is incorporated into the peninsula with a snack bar on the family room side.

GETTING CENTERED

Designing a kitchen is very much like planning a space shot or any other large endeavor. Looked at in its entirety, it can seem overwhelming. But if you divide the job into smaller, more manageable elements, the whole project falls together naturally and logically. What are the key elements in a kitchen? You may have noticed on the preceding pages that we often refer to a kitchen's parts not by the usual component names—sink, range, refrigerator, and so forth—but rather by the functions they serve. Looking at your kitchen as a series of interrelated "centers" helps organize your thinking. First let's examine the three centers most experts regard as essential: then, on pages 72 and 73, we'll discuss three more you should consider.

CLEANING

At the sink you normally clean food before it's prepared, and dishes afterward. Combine the sink with counter space on either side, a disposer, a dishwasher, and possibly a trash compactor and you have a center that accommodates all your cleaning chores. Each of these tasks and items requires a minimum amount of space.

Right-handers should allot at least 30 inches of counter space to the right of the sink, 24 inches to the left. Left-handers, of course, should reverse these specifications.

A dishwasher requires a 24-inch-wide space; a trash compactor fits into the space of a 15-inch cabinet. You will also need 24 to 30 inches of clearance in front of these appliances to open the dishwasher door and to pull out the trash compactor receptacle.

A cleaning center gains in efficiency with the right kind of storage. You'll need space for:
• Bowls, strainers, and cutlery used in preparation of fruits and vegetables.
• Non-refrigerated foods that require washing.
• Dishwasher detergent and other kitchen cleaning supplies (possibly in a locked cabinet if you have small children).
• Everyday dishes and glassware. Since the dishwasher is located here, you'll save yourself steps if the tableware you use most often is stored near the cleaning center.

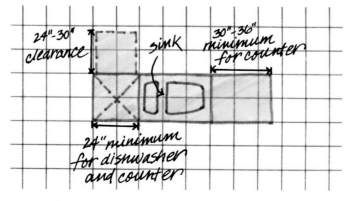

COOLING

Locate your cooling/food-storage center near the kitchen entrance to save carrying grocery sacks farther than necessary.

Refrigerators with top or bottom freezers measure 28 to 30 inches in width. Side-by-side units come in 30-, 33-, and 36-inch widths. On some models, doors can be hinged to open right or left.

Plan at least 18 inches of counter space on the door-opening side of the refrigerator, and allow enough space to open doors more than 90 degrees for easy shelf removal.

A refrigerator with an automatic ice maker or cold water dispenser needs a convenient connection to water lines.

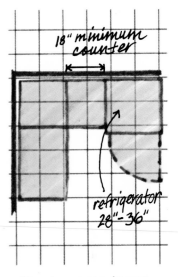

Store beverages, freezer-wrap, and cold-storage containers in this center.

(continued)

COOKING

Whether your cooking center incorporates a drop-in range, a slip-in range/oven, a freestanding range, or a cooktop and built-in oven, your space requirements are the same. You'll need 18 inches of heatproof counter material on either side of your cooking surface. And if you have a built-in oven, you'll need 15 inches of counter space on the working side of the unit. The overall size of your cooking center will depend on the size of the appliance you choose.

Freestanding ranges are available in 30- and 36-inch widths. Cooktops vary in width from 30 to 46 inches, with a separate 18-inch grill available. Wall ovens measure 27 to 30 inches in width.

Other requirements for your cooking center are:
• A ventilating hood and fan.
• Storage for pots, pans, cooking utensils, and serving pieces. Pullout drawers or racks are handiest for saucepans and skillets. A popular cabinet-saving strategy is to hang cookware overhead.
• Storage for food seasonings.

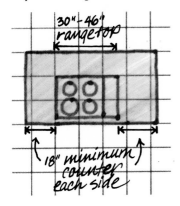

PLANNING

A ny kitchen with a few extra feet of floor space can benefit from a planning center. Minimum dimensions for an effective desk area are a width of 24 inches and a depth of 54 inches (24 inches for the desk surface, and 30 inches for clearance to pull out a chair).

Locate your planning center in a part of your kitchen away from main work and activity areas, and provide adequate lighting for paper work. For the desk, purchase or build a unit that incorporates storage for essentials such as cook books, a telephone, and writing supplies.

The desk surface should be 30 inches from the floor (6 inches lower than standard counter height in the rest of the kitchen). Its top surface should be smooth and easy to maintain, but not shiny; reflected light fatigues eyes.

Knee space is essential in any desk. You'll want drawer space, but don't let an apron drawer cut into your knee space. You might instead consider a freestanding drawer unit or a two-drawer file cabinet placed under an open desktop. This arrangement provides ample storage, plus necessary leg room.

Other items to consider for your planning center are:
• A clock.
• An electrical outlet.
• Specialized storage for records, recipes, and supplies.
• A bulletin board.
• A home computer. Even if you're not planning to invest in a computer right away, you'd be wise to allow additional space for one. There may be a computer in your future, and a kitchen planning center is the logical place for it. (To learn more about home computers, see pages 114 and 115.)

MICROWAVE

L ocate your microwave oven near your conventional cooking center, or give it a mini-center of its own. If you opt for a separate center, here are some things you'll want to consider.

Microwave units come in both counter-top and built-in models. Dimensions vary widely among different manufacturers, with depths of 14, 16, and 18 inches, and widths of 20, 21, 25, and 27 inches the most common. Besides size, also consider how your unit's door opens. Some swing like left-hinged refrigerator doors; others open from top to bottom the way conventional ovens do. Be sure to allow sufficient clearance in whatever direction your door swings.

If you've chosen a built-in microwave, position it at a comfortable height—generally eye level. Built-in models require some space around them for air circulation.

Whether built-in or countertop, plan for 15 to 18 inches of

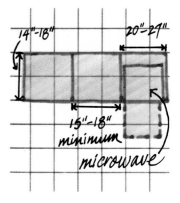

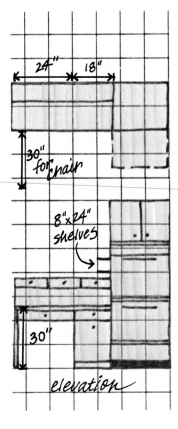

24" 18"

30" for chair

8"x24" shelves

30"

elevation

BAKING

A baking/mixing center is essential in any kitchen. But just how far you want to go here depends largely on the amount of baking your family does. If baking is high on your list of culinary achievements, you'll want to plan a complete baking center with specialized storage and all of the convenience features you can build into it.

Locate your baking/mixing center near either the oven or the refrigerator, or ideally, between these two appliances.

You'll need at least 36 inches of counter top for adequate work space. And working here will be more comfortable if the surface is slightly lower than the rest of your counters—6 or 7 inches below elbow height. The lower height makes mixing and kneading less tiring. This means you'll need 32- to 33-inch-high base cabinets.

Treat yourself to a ceramic or marble counter-top insert for rolling pastry. The counter should be extra-deep—30 inches—so you'll have plenty of room for rolling out dough. And add under-cabinet lights so you're never working in your own shadow.

Plan storage in your baking center to include space for these items:
• Cook books. You'll also want to have space and a rack to hold the cook book or recipe from which you're working.
• Mixing bowls and baking utensils.
• Baking pans. Store cookie sheets and rectangular cake pans vertically in compartmented cabinets that let you slip these items in on their sides, rather than in stacks.
• A heat-resistant surface for setting down items hot from the oven, and a baker's rack

for cooling them.
• Sugar, flour, and spices.
• Small appliances for mixing or baking, such as a mixer, blender, or food processor. With proper planning, you can store these appliances in the area between base and top cabinets. In the baking center shown here, sliding doors cover this appliance "garage."
• Specialty cookware such as holiday baking equipment, shaped cake pans, or other items you use infrequently.

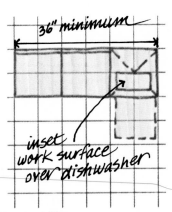

36" minimum

inset work surface over dishwasher

counter surface adjacent to your microwave oven. The built-in microwave shown *at left* has space both to the side and above for incoming and outgoing dishes.

Since microwave cooking has introduced a whole collection of specialized cookware, plan storage space for these pieces near your oven—built-in drawers as shown here, or cabinet space you might designate below or above your counter top.

CREATING
EATING SPACE

Tight space always presents the biggest obstacle to creating a kitchen eating area—but don't let the inch pinch stop you from giving it a try. Just a small plan modification might make room for a table and chairs. If not, consider a snack counter with stools that tuck underneath, or a booth with stationary seating. Study these and the next two pages to determine which arrangement would work best in your kitchen.

Whether or not you opt for a table with chairs depends on your floor space and the number of family members who will eat in the kitchen. Plan 12 to 15 square feet of floor space for each person. That allows space for the table, chairs, and the people themselves. In other words, a family of four needs a minimum of 48 square feet of floor space for kitchen dining.

This space requirement is really very difficult to cheat. You may be able to gain a few inches by placing your table and chairs at an angle as shown in the lower drawing *at right*. But don't try paring down the size of the table itself; plan 21 to 24 inches of table space for each adult.

You also should factor in space for serving around the table. If that's your plan, place the table 44 inches from adjacent walls.

Locate your eating space away from traffic routes. For easy serving, place the table and chairs near cooking and food preparation centers. And if you'd rather shorten your steps after dinner, try for close proximity to the cleanup center, too.

Contemplating a total remodeling or an addition? If so, think through how much time your family might spend around a kitchen table. It might also be a spot for homework and an after-school snack or informal entertaining. If your life-style is such that this could be more than just a spot for eating family meals, it might be worthwhile to cut back in some other area to gain the dining space you need.

(continued)

SEATING ALLOWANCES

People need space, too. Here are some guidelines for placing tables, chairs, and diners.

A seated person needs 32 inches to rise from the table. That's an absolute minimum. To be on the safe side, figure 36 inches between table and wall; 44 inches if you serve around the table.

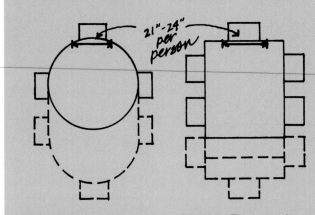

Calculate the maximum size of your table with extensions and additional chairs. Be flexible and shift table positions as we have in our drawings. This may give you the extra inches you need to make full use of both furniture and kitchen space.

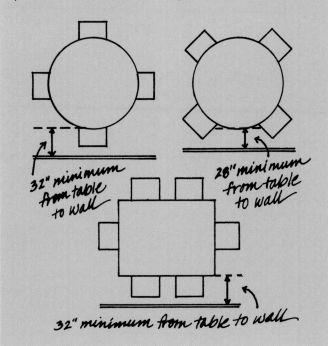

CREATING
EATING SPACE
(continued)

COUNTERS AND STOOLS

The best way to incorporate eating space into the core of a kitchen is to install a counter, and you have a wide variety of types, shapes, and sizes to choose from.

To determine the length of your counter, multiply the number of persons who will be eating at one time by the 21-inch minimum of table space each adult requires.

Eating counters may be part of a peninsula or freestanding island, and they may be one of three heights.

If you prefer a table-height counter, it should be 28 to 32 inches from the floor. This counter requires 18-inch-high chairs and 20 inches of leg room between the chair front and the vertical surface under the counter.

Or you can make your eating counter the same height as the rest of the kitchen counters. This 36-inch-high counter requires 24-inch-high bar stools, and allows 24 inches for knee space.

You also can go up to bar height—42 to 45 inches from the floor. Here you need 30-inch-high bar stools with foot rests. This height works best in situations where the eating area backs a range or sink. Elevating the eating surface above the work surface also provides protection from spatters and splashes.

Don't feel restrained in the design of your eating counter. It needn't be rectangular or surfaced with the same material as the other counter tops in the kitchen. If an angled or curved layout gives you more space and suits the design of your kitchen, go ahead and use it.

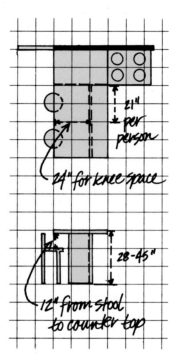

BOOTHS

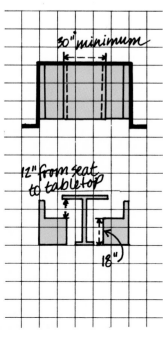

The architecture of your kitchen might make a booth your best bet for eating space. An alcove, a jog in the wall, or a recessed window could be a starting place. But you don't need an architectural excuse to install a booth. In lots of cases where space simply won't allow chairs to be moved into or away from a table, a built-in eating space is the answer.

To determine the dimensions of the booth's table surface, figure 21 inches of table length for each person and at least 15 inches of depth. For instance, a family of four would require a surface 30 inches deep and 42 inches long. Though the table might be acceptable for dining if it were less than 30 inches deep, it would cramp the leg room of diners seated across from each other.

With the eating surface at standard table height of 28 to 30 inches, the seating units, or banquettes, should be 18 inches high and as long as the table surface. Install banquettes so their front edges are positioned 3 or 4 inches "into" the table surface as shown in the drawing *at left*.

Depending on space and the size of your family, you may want to install a U-shaped booth with seating on three sides. The same space requirements for a standard two-bench booth apply.

WHAT YOU NEED TO KNOW ABOUT CONSTRUCTION, PLUMBING, AND WIRING

Neglect to figure out what's going on inside your kitchen's walls and even best-laid plans could go awry—or hopelessly over budget. Generally speaking, you can knock out walls and juggle components to your heart's content; the catch is that some changes are far more costly than others, and a few are mechanically impossible. So before you fix on any one of the many possible layouts you can generate with graph paper and kitchen cutouts, let's examine some facts about a kitchen's lifelines.

A person can live in a house for years without knowing (or needing to know) how water travels to and from the kitchen sink, the structural importance of a kitchen's walls, or the hidden pathways electricity and heat follow. Call in a remodeling contractor, though, and these are among the first things he'll want to determine.

Our anatomy drawing, *opposite,* along with some sleuthing on your part, can help you get the jump on him—and find out in advance if your plans are practical or even feasible.

Start with the sink

Of all a kitchen's fixtures, the sink is perhaps the most fixed, and the most difficult to relocate. The problem lies not so much with the sink itself, nor even with its hot and cold *supply lines;* these are relatively easy to extend in just about any direction.

Drainage is a different matter. Look under your sink and you'll see a *trap* that looks something like the one pictured. Water collected in the trap provides a seal that prevents sewer gases from backing up into your kitchen.

The trap in turn connects to a vertical run of piping inside the wall. Waste water from the sink drops down the *drain* below the point where the trap hooks in; piping above that point serves as a *vent* that carries off sewer gases and also lets air into the system to promote drainage. Your sink's trap may be directly connected to the same *stack* that drains and vents other fixtures in the house, or it may hook in via a system of *branches,* as illustrated in our drawing.

Plumbing codes (and good drainage) limit the distance a trap may be located from its drain/vent lines. The actual span varies somewhat from one locality to another, but generally speaking, you can't move a sink more than 3 to 4 feet without either adding or extending branch lines; in some situations you may need an entirely new run of piping from basement to roof. Modifying lines inside your walls ups the plumbing bill, of course, and usually calls for carpentry work as well.

Which walls hold up your house?

Speaking of carpentry, do you know how your kitchen's walls fit into your home's overall structure? Some walls serve merely as *partitions* separating interior spaces; these walls bear no structural responsibility for what's above, and are known as *non-bearing.* Non-bearing walls are relatively easy and inexpensive to remove, provided they don't carry drain and vent lines.

Bearing walls, on the other hand, support the roof or floor above. To remove a bearing wall, a contractor has to add a beam or some other alternative support system. You'll pay a premium for the extra work and materials.

About the only physical difference between a bearing and non-bearing wall is that the former has a double *top plate,* as shown in our drawing. This you might be able to identify by drilling a small hole in the wall a few inches from the point where it meets the ceiling. Better yet, journey to the basement or attic and note the direction *floor joists* run. Bearing walls always run perpendicular to joists; non-bearing are usually parallel.

While you're in the basement or attic, pinpoint the location of your home's plumbing stack and any branches that run off it.

Getting gas to a range

Compared to water pipes, gas lines are simple, and relatively easy for a plumber to relocate. A single line runs from the meter to the range, and possibly to other appliances as well. Some localities permit range hookups with a special *flexible connector.* These come in differing lengths, which means you can shift your range a few feet in one direction or another without modifying the gas line. Other communities require a solid hookup—a bit more costly to provide.

Making electrical changes

The trouble with altering the wiring in a kitchen—especially an older one—is that you usually face an all-or-nothing proposition. Most codes stipulate that the entire system be brought up to present-day standards any time a change is made, so you may as well brace yourself for a complete overhaul, and possibly the additional expense of bringing in more power to your home's main service panel.

The silver lining here is that an electrician can snake new lines just about anywhere, leaving you plenty of freedom in locating receptacles, lights, and appliances. And of course you also benefit from the safety and convenience of an up-to-date electrical system.

What about heat outlets?

For clarity's sake we've eliminated heating equipment from our drawing. Electric baseboard units are the easiest to relocate. Moving hot water or steam radiators calls for moderately simple re-piping, and usually can be done by the same tradesman who handles your plumbing. Forced-air heating or cooling registers may require sheet-metal as well as carpentry work.

INSIDE A KITCHEN'S WALLS

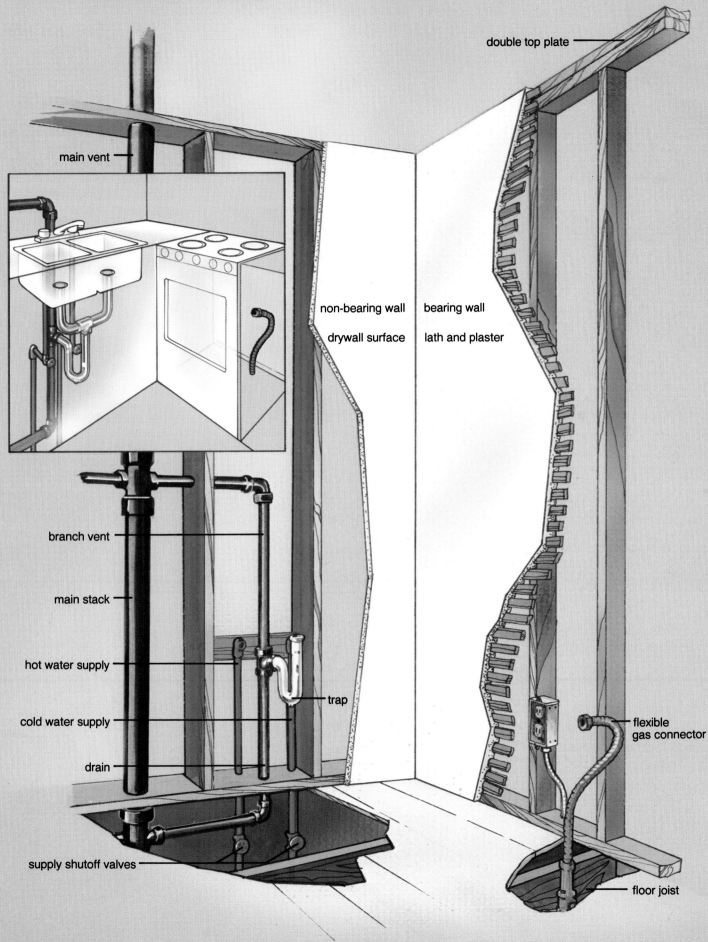

double top plate

main vent

non-bearing wall   bearing wall

drywall surface   lath and plaster

branch vent

main stack

hot water supply

cold water supply

drain

trap

flexible gas connector

supply shutoff valves

floor joist

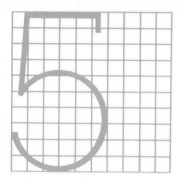

SELECTING KITCHEN COMPONENTS

Your kitchen can only be as good as the sum of its parts. So when it's time to buy a major appliance or other component, make sure it earns its keep. This chapter points you in the right direction with shopping guidelines for everything from a combination range to the kitchen sink. But you should be prepared to do some homework of your own and ask sharp questions about each appliance you consider. The more you can learn about what's available, the better your chances of buying an appliance you'll be happy with for years.

EVALUATING YOUR OPTIONS

Kitchen planners will tell you that, on the average, a family should plan to budget as much for a kitchen remodeling as they would for a new car. Given that kind of expenditure, you can appreciate why you need to evaluate every option and component with a critical eye.

Start by being realistic about how much you can spend, then vow to stick to your budget. That step alone will help you sort out the appliances (and their features) that are necessities from the ones that are merely niceties.

If you're outfitting your kitchen from the floor covering up, you can afford to splurge a little on one component, and buy a lower-priced model of another. But if you're making a single purchase—such as upgrading your microwave oven —you'll have less leeway.

A good place to start comparison shopping for a particular appliance is your public library. There you'll find a variety of consumer publications that give brand-name ratings of the appliances you need. You'll also learn quite a bit about the range of features available, and what they cost. This information alone will make you a better-informed shopper than 90 percent of the consumers in dealer showrooms. Take notes, and try to narrow your choices down to a few specific brands and models that offer the features you want at a price you can afford.

A few calls to the appliance dealers listed in the Yellow Pages will tell you where to find the models on your list —and some dealers may even quote prices over the phone. In deciding which dealers you'll actually visit, you may want to get friends' recommendations and check with your local Better Business Bureau.

Is the price right?
Your lowest price quote may not in fact be your best deal. Generous credit terms or appliance trade-in allowances may make another dealer's slightly higher price more attractive overall.

Find out, too, the extent of each dealer's/appliance's warranty coverage. Which parts are warranted? Does the warranty include labor? And will the warranty be honored by another dealer if you move?

When you compare specific appliances, consider their operating costs as well as the purchase price. Energy guides attached to all major appliances estimate their energy cost on a yearly basis. If an appliance features an energy-saving option—such as an automatic ignition instead of a pilot light on a gas range—find out what you're paying for that option. It may be worth the added cost if it has a short "payback period"—the time in which your estimated energy savings add up to the cost of the option.

Bringing it home
If an appliance needs professional installation, find out if it's included in the purchase price, and work out an acceptable delivery and installation schedule. If you decide to do the work yourself, make sure that installation charges aren't included in the price you're paying. And see that you have all pertinent instructions and special tools on hand.

After you've been a smart shopper, be a smart owner. Return any warranty registration forms and keep your copy of the warranty and sales receipt in a central "kitchen appliance" file. Finally, to avoid costly service calls, read your owner's manual and follow its recommendations.

SINKS

SINGLE-BOWL SINK

with a dishwasher, has a 22x25x8-inch basin. It's large enough to soak big pots and pans, yet doesn't waste precious counter space.

A *double-bowl sink* makes sense for a kitchen that doesn't have an automatic dishwasher. It needs a slightly wider 22x33-inch space, but its two identically sized basins can handle food preparation and dish washing chores simultaneously.

A *triple-bowl sink* features two standard-size basins plus a smaller disposer basin in between. This unit, which measures 22x43 inches, works well in larger kitchens or in kitchens with more than one active cook. The center-well disposer corrals scraps while you prepare food or wash dishes in the side bowls.

For each of these sink configurations, you can buy op-

TRIPLE-BOWL SINK

N o kitchen component does more jobs more often than the sink. Here's where most meals begin and end, with many a side trip during the cooking and serving processes in between. When you shop for a new sink, its material, size, shape, and color are just some of the variables you need to consider to get the sink that's right for your kitchen.

The material difference
Stainless steel sinks are lightweight and therefore easy to install, stain-resistant, and durable. Their satin or brushed finishes also keep their good looks through routine wear. Before buying a stainless sink, check the gauge or thickness of the steel—18- to 20-gauge steel is satisfactory. Also compare the nickel and chrome content of various models. Nickel helps prevent corrosion; chrome enhances the finish. The more of both, the better.

Enameled cast iron sinks are heavy, but they resist acids, stains, scratches, and chips and dents, and they come in a rainbow of colors. *Enamel-on-steel sinks* look a lot like enameled cast iron sinks but they aren't as heavy or wear-resistant. Generally, they cost less, too.

Shapes and sizes
The *single-bowl sink,* a good choice for a kitchen equipped

IMPORTED SINK

SINK WITH SIDE DISPOSER

CORNER SINK

tional hardwood cutting boards that fit over the basins to extend your counter space. Some manufacturers also offer wooden drainboards for the large bowls.

An *imported sink* combines avant-garde form and multipurpose function. The curvaceous model shown here features two large circular basins that can be fitted with a wooden cutting board and a plasticized wire draining basket. A food strainer fits over the smaller basin in the center.

The *extra-deep sink,* about 13½ inches square and 15½ inches deep, excels in small kitchens and family rooms, and in homes without a separate laundry room. The depth of the basin makes it equally suitable for bathing a baby or repotting plants.

A *sink with a side disposer* occupies the same space as a

double-bowl sink, but uses it for two different-size basins—a big one for dishwashing and a smaller one for food preparation. The small basin's shallow depth lets you install a disposer without changing the drainpipe, and frees more space inside the base cabinet.

A *corner sink's* L shape lets you install a double- or triple-bowl sink in a counter area that might otherwise be underused. Use one 13½x16-inch basin for dishwashing, the other for food preparation.

A *bar or party sink* provides more convenience than you might think. Of course, it's handy when you entertain. But you'll also find it useful when there's more than one cook in the kitchen. A family with children can easily use an auxiliary sink like this one as a beverage center, potting sink, or wash-up station.

Installation and accessory options

Your new sink mounts to the counter top in either of two ways, depending on its type. Self-rimming sinks are easiest to install because they seal directly to the counter top.

They're easy to clean, too, because they leave fewer places for kitchen grime to collect around the sink rim. Rimmed types use a flat metal band between the sink and the counter surface.

Faucets and handles (called "brass fittings" in the trade) sometimes come with the sink, other times must be purchased separately. Some have colored handle inserts to complement your decorating scheme. Choose easy-to-grip fittings and accessories that operate well with wet slippery hands. Here are your options.

Single-control faucets let you fine-tune water temperature and flow with just one hand. They're available in satin and polished chrome finishes.

Swiveling spray spouts for faucets and hose sprays make rinsing produce and dishes a breeze. They'll send a shower into all corners of the sink.

Strainers help prevent clogs by trapping food particles before they slip down the drain.

Pop-up drains save you the trouble of fishing in scalding dishwater to release the sink stopper. A handle mounted at the back of the sink top opens and closes the drain.

Soap and lotion dispensers help cut the clutter around the sink. These pump-type dispensers fit into the back deck area of the sink.

EXTRA-DEEP SINK

BAR SINK

REFRIGERATORS AND FREEZERS

SINGLE-DOOR REFRIGERATOR

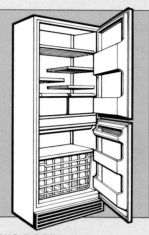

TWO-DOOR REFRIGERATOR

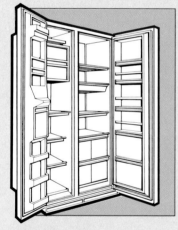

SIDE-BY-SIDE REFRIGERATOR

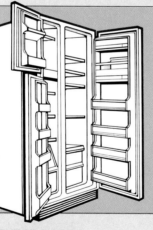

THREE-DOOR SIDE-BY-SIDE

Bigger isn't necessarily better (or more efficient) when it comes to refrigerators. Refrigerators are expensive to purchase and operate, so don't pay for more storage space than you need. As a rule of thumb, buy 12 cubic feet of total storage space (refrigerator and freezer) for the first two members of your family, and two more cubic feet for each additional person.

Measure the space where you want to locate your refrigerator, then shop for a model that fits. Check installation requirements; some models need breathing room along the top, back, or sides that you'll need to allow for.

Choosing a style

Now it's time to use the figures for storage capacity and kitchen floor space to choose the style of refrigerator that's right for you.

A *single-door refrigerator* puts some limits on the amount of food you can keep —especially in the freezer. The most basic model of this style has a small freezer compartment that holds only about a week's worth of frozen foods. Although economical to buy and operate, this style must be defrosted manually. And freezer temperature usually isn't low enough for long-term storage.

A *two-door refrigerator* usually has its freezer unit at the top or bottom. Unlike freezers in most one-door models, these freezers are fine for long-term storage. Some defrost manually, but most are totally frost-free.

The *side-by-side refrigerator* is another popular two- or three-door style. Easy access to food is the drawing card here, but the necessarily narrower shelves won't let you store extremely bulky items, such as a large frozen turkey.

Options and standard features

You can customize most of these refrigerator styles with a variety of features, each one of which ups the final price tag. Here are some of the most popular options.

Automatic ice makers end the hassles of refilllng ice cube trays and running out of ice. But they require a run of plumbing to supply the ice maker with water, so be sure to figure its installation cost into the total purchase price of the refrigerator.

Cold beverage dispensers and/or ice cube dispensers on the outside of the refrigerator door are not only convenient, they're also energy-efficient: you don't waste cooled air by opening the door.

Dual temperature controls are standard on most refrigerator/freezers. But separate temperature controls also may be available for vegetable bins, meat keepers, and even the butter compartment.

Decorator door panels give you greater leeway in harmonizing your refrigerator with your kitchen decor. Some door panels are interchangeable to let you redecorate your refrigerator along with the rest of your kitchen.

Adding freezer capacity

When it's time to invest in a separate freezer, select a sensible size. Three or four cubic feet of freezer space for each person in your family is a good yardstick. Remember, operating a freezer at less than two-thirds of its capacity is false economy.

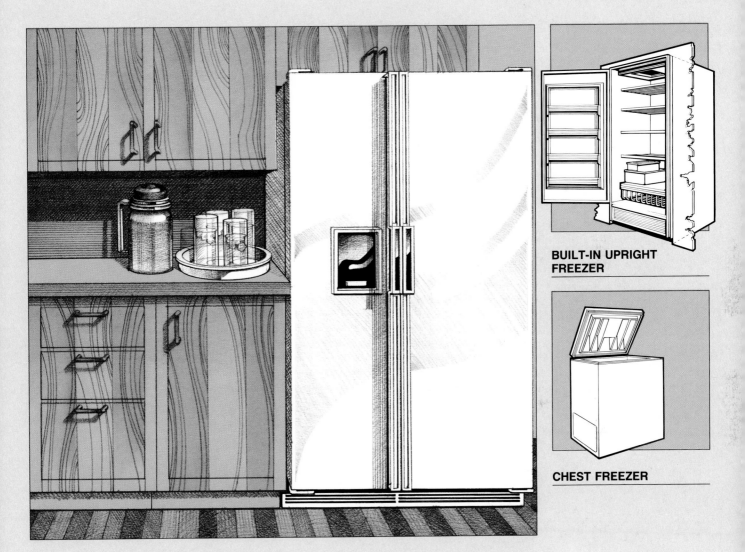

BUILT-IN UPRIGHT FREEZER

CHEST FREEZER

Top-opening *chest freezers,* usually less expensive than upright models, are often more economical to operate, too. Because cold air sinks, chest freezers don't lose as much cooled air when they're opened as upright models do. Most chest freezers require manual defrosting, but with less frequency than manual-defrost upright models.

Upright freezers come in both frost-free and manual-defrost models. Shelves in upright freezers make them more convenient for organizing your frozen food inventory; there's no digging or heavy lifting when you need to retrieve a package. Upright freezers also occupy less floor space.

Both chest and upright models are available with some or all of these popular options.

A *"power on" light* on the freezer cabinet quickly indicates whether or not the unit is working. If a freezer malfunctions or is accidentally turned off, you could lose a costly investment in groceries.

Frost-free options on some models eliminate the need for manual defrosting.

Water drains on some manual-defrost freezers simplify defrosting chores.

A door lock can prevent pilferage if you keep your freezer in an unlocked area, such as a garage.

Organizers such as baskets and juice-can racks are available for upright models to maximize storage space and ease food retrieval.

OVENS, COOKTOPS, AND RANGES

Today you have more ways to cook your food than ever before. There's an ever-increasing number of ovens, cooktops, and ranges for you to choose from. Before you start shopping for one, though, assess what you like and dislike about your present cooking equipment, then make a near-future projection of your family's cooking and entertaining needs. Also, be sure to evaluate the space limitations in your kitchen.

Next, decide what form of energy you'll use—gas or electricity. (For coal- and wood-burning ranges, see page 88.) Check with your local utility for rate comparisons, and switch fuels only if substantial savings are involved (or only if you're strongly committed to the cooking characteristics of another fuel—if you're buying a gas-only restaurant range, for instance).

Your utility's home service department is your best source of information on fuel types, availability, and costs. Whether it recommends electricity or natural gas, you'll have the following appliance options when you start to shop.

MICROWAVE/GAS/ CONVECTION RANGE

SLIDE-IN RANGE

Cooking appliance configurations

A *freestanding range* rests on the floor as a self-contained unit, with burners on the top and the oven below. These ranges have a normal width of 30 inches, although 24- and 36-inch-wide models also are made. The cooking surface is positioned at the standard 36-inch counter-top height, but on some freestanding ranges with an upper oven, it may be lower; the cooktop depth is usually 27 inches. Freestanding ranges usually offer easy-to-clean backsplashes and roomy bottom drawers or broilers.

The *over/under double-oven range* squeezes a lot of cooking convenience into a 30-inch space. Most manufacturers recommend fitting a specially designed, box-shaped ventilator hood atop the upper oven.

A *slide-in range* is simply a freestanding range without side panels; the whole unit fits snugly between your kitchen cabinets. You can install an optional backsplash, or right or left side panel if one side will be exposed.

A *drop-in or built-in range* has surface burners and an oven below. This model, also usually 30 inches wide, is permanently installed in kitchen cabinets and usually rests on a wood base. The drop-in range is well-suited for installation in a center island since there's no backsplash to interrupt the surface. Without a bottom drawer, it puts the broiler conveniently at waist level.

A *cooktop* is built right into the counter top. The 24- to 36-inch-wide surface has two to six heating units or burners.

A *built-in oven* frees cabinet space by hiding in a wall. Double built-in ovens install one unit over the other, or side by side. Units come in 24- and 30-inch widths.

A *convection oven* can cook at lower temperatures and in

less time because a blower forces the heated air around the food.

A *microwave oven*—portable, built-in, or part of a freestanding range—uses high-frequency radio waves to cook food directly without heating the surrounding air.

Some unusual combinations
Energy-efficient gas ranges replace constantly burning pilot lights with electric or electronic (pilotless) ignition systems, which use no gas.

A *combination microwave oven and conventional oven* (or microwave and convection oven) offers the convenience of using each cooking method separately or both at the same time. When you use the two together, microwaves speed cooking, and heat from the

conventional or convection oven browns the food.

Glass ceramic cooktops are energy-efficient and easy-to-clean alternatives to regular electric burners. Manufacturers recommend the use of flat-bottomed pots and pans to maximize heat transfer. Because the glass ceramic surface cools slowly, you can turn off the heat a few minutes before food is done.

Magnetic induction cooktops work only with iron or steel utensils. The units cook evenly and efficiently without ever getting hot. Cleanup is easy because the cooking surface remains cool.

A potpourri of options
Choose from this list according to your family's cooking routine—and budget.
• Built-in barbecues, griddles, cutting boards, warmer shelves, and exhaust fans.
• Self-cleaning ovens that use a high-temperature cleaning cycle to "burn" spills into a fine ash you can sponge off.
• Continuous cleaning ovens with interior surfaces that dissolve most soil while you bake.
• Variable-speed broilers.
• Warming ovens.
• Thermostatically controlled heating units.
• Continuously adjustable heat controls.

BUILT-IN COOKTOP

RANGE WITH INTERCHANGEABLE COOKING CARTRIDGES

• Interchangeable surface cartridges such as grills, smooth tops, standard electric units, rotisseries, shish kabobs, griddles, and French fryers.
• Lighted control panels, ovens, and temperature and time indicators.
• Oven rotisseries.
• Delay cook-hold oven controls you can set to turn on at a predetermined time.
• Meat thermometers attached to the inside of the oven.
• Child-proof controls.
• Surface temperature limits.
• Decorator appliance colors and interchangeable oven-door panels.

The new waves
As microwave technology advances, so do the innovations in microwave ovens. When comparison shopping, remember that the power output (in watts) affects cooking speed. Powerful microwave ovens with outputs of 650 or more watts cook food 75 percent faster than a conventional oven; economy units of 400 watts cook 60 percent faster.

Any unit that you purchase should have a push-to-start control, a secure door lock, an indicator light, and an end-of-cycle signal.

OVER/UNDER DOUBLE-OVEN RANGE

RESTAURANT AND COAL- OR WOOD-BURNING RANGES

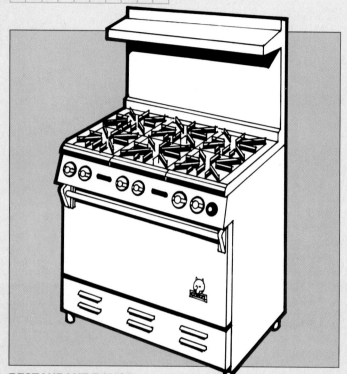

RESTAURANT RANGE

COAL/WOOD/ELECTRIC RANGE

If you're a serious cook, you should consider a *restaurant range* for your kitchen. Nothing else offers a restaurant range's combination of large capacity, accurate temperature control, and durability.

You have a considerable choice of restaurant ranges, both gas and electric. Widths vary from 23 inches to 68 inches, and depth is usually at least 6 inches greater than that of conventional freestanding ranges.

The range illustrated *above* is one of the most basic gas types. It's outfitted with six burners and one extra-wide oven. Some of the wider models are equipped with as many as 12 burners and two extra-wide ovens. All burners on the model shown are 11 inches in diameter to handle large frying pans and stock pots. Other restaurant range options include griddles, combination

broiler/griddles at cooktop level, and broilers mounted above the cooktop.

Though not as common as their gas counterparts, electric restaurant ranges also are available in many sizes and configurations. High-speed coil elements are options, as are griddles. In lieu of an elevated storage shelf, some models come equipped with an elevated broiler.

If you decide to invest in a restaurant range—and it's a considerable investment—pinpoint the space you have available and assess your cooking needs. Look for a medium-size model, unless you do a lot of large-scale cooking. Only a few models are equipped with self-cleaning ovens. You won't have much choice about finish, either— they usually come in only black or stainless steel.

When you've narrowed your choice down to one or two models, measure your doorways to make sure the range you want will move through them. Also, since restaurant ranges weigh considerably more than consumer models, check your floor supports; you may need additional bracing. And ask about your unit's installation and ventilation requirements. For example, you may have to fireproof the wall behind the range, or install larger ¾-inch gas supply lines.

Coal or wood, plus electricity

If you'd like the character of a coal- or wood-burning cookstove in your kitchen but don't want to sacrifice the convenience of a modern range, a combination coal/wood/electric range may be your choice. It combines an electric range and a wood- or coal-burning

cookstove in a 35-inch-wide unit, letting you use the cooking mode that suits you best.

The model shown *above* contains a malleable iron coal- or wood-heated cooktop in addition to four electric surface units; the oven is completely electric.

There's also at least one model that comes equipped with a combination oven that heats conventionally or with coal or wood. It includes a built-in coal- or wood-burning kitchen heater as well. Vents in the side allow heated air to circulate throughout the kitchen.

The ranges now in production have wood- or coal-burning units on the left side and electric elements and ovens on the right. *Only* the right side, where electric elements are located, can be installed next to a cabinet.

DISHWASHERS

The main concern about a dishwasher used to be "Will it really get my dishes clean?" Now that dishwashers have proved themselves, the question has become "What type of dishwasher should I buy, and what features do I want?"

You have only two basic types to consider. *Built-in models* are designed for permanent installation below a counter top, close to plumbing lines. *Portable models* roll from a storage area to the sink as needed. They attach to the water faucet and drain through the sink. Both types typically measure 24 inches wide, 24 inches deep, and 35 inches high; most load from the front.

Some portable units offer you the option of building them in at a later date by means of an optional conversion kit. For other special installations, you can get a compact 18-inch-wide dishwasher, a space-

making dishwasher-sink combination equipped with a garbage disposer, and a dishwasher/range combination.

Here are some additional points to consider and features to look for.
- *Capacity.* Choose a model that's big enough for a day's worth of your family's dirty dishes.
- *Loading flexibility.* Many models offer adjustable dish racks and removable flatware baskets.
- *Durability.* Check the interior and the door lining carefully, and make sure they are made from a rust-, scratch-, and stain-resistant material. Common lining materials include porcelain enamel, stainless steel, vinyl-coated steel, and various plastics.
- *Strainer/filtering system.* Strainer plates in the bottoms of units keep bits of food from clogging the drain. In some models, a self-cleaning filter

BUILT-IN DISHWASHER

PORTABLE DISHWASHER

BUILT-IN UNDER-SINK DISHWASHER

removes tiny particles of food during the wash cycle; a backwash system then cleans the filter and flushes food down the drain.
- *Soft-food disposer.* This option liquefies soft foods for disposal into waste water; you don't need to prerinse dirty dishes in the sink.
- *Detergent and rinse additive dispensers.* These dispensers automatically release detergent and rinse additives at the proper times.
- *Preheating cycles.* Some dishwashers have a preheater that saves energy by letting you operate your water heater at a lower temperature.
- *Decorator kits.* Many manufacturers now offer decorator panels and trim kits to match your kitchen's color scheme.
- *Additional features* on portable models include faucet connectors that let you use running water while the dishwasher is operating, a retractable cord, easy-rolling casters, and a cutting-board top.
- As you move up manufacturers' lines, you'll find an increasing number of these dishwashing cycles.
- A *regular cycle* cleans normally soiled dishes.
- A *quick cycle* provides a short wash for lightly soiled dishes.

- A *gentle (or china/crystal) cycle* aerates the water to soften its force.
- A *heavy-duty cycle* extends the normal cycle or adds an extra wash cycle for tough jobs.
- A *soak/scrub (or pots and pans) cycle* briefly wets the dishes, then a soaking solution softens the food before regular washing.
- A *power-saver cycle* conserves energy by letting dishes air-dry rather than using the heating element. Sometimes the power-saver cycle also bypasses the heat booster that maintains a minimum water temperature during washing.
- A *sanitizing cycle* heats water to a factory-set temperature to sanitize dishes.
- A *rinse-and-hold cycle* rinses dishes in a short, no-detergent cycle. This prevents food from souring and drying on dishes while a full dishwasher load accumulates.
- A *delay-wash cycle* available on some models allows you to program your dishwasher to begin the wash cycle up to nine hours after you set the controls.
- A *dish-warmer cycle* lets you take advantage of the drying stage of the regular cycle to preheat dishes for serving hot foods at mealtime.

DISPOSERS AND COMPACTORS

DISPOSERS

Consider these features when you shop for a compactor.
- A *removable rammer* to simplify cleanup.
- A *key-activated on/off switch* for added safety.
- A *"toe touch" door latch* that allows you to open the unit when your arms are full.
- An *automatic air filter or deodorizer.*
- *Decorator panels* or trim kits that complement your decor.
- *Special collection bags.* If a compactor you're considering requires them, find out their cost and where they're sold.

Garbage disposers
A garbage disposer cuts, shreds, and grinds food wastes, letting you simply flush them down the drain.

Batch-feed disposers grind from 1½ to 2 quarts of waste at a time. They're controlled by a built-in switch activated by replacing the drain lid. The *continuous-feed disposer* is usually controlled by a wall switch. It allows you to continuously feed waste into the disposer as it operates.

When you shop, look for features like these.
- A *sturdy motor,* preferably ½ horsepower or greater.
- *Corrosion-resistant parts.*
- An *overload protector.*
- *Automatic reversing action* of the blades to help free jams.
- *Noise insulation.*

TRASH COMPACTORS

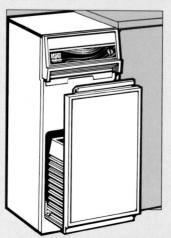

A trash compactor can cut the problem of kitchen trash down to size. With a compactor, a family of four can compress a week's accumulated trash (including bottles, cartons, paper, plastics, and other dry food waste) into one bagful or bucketful.

You can choose from built-in, freestanding, and convertible styles designed to fit under a counter, and varying in size from 12 to 18 inches wide.

WASHERS
AND
DRYERS

As our life-styles change, so does our clothing—and so also does the equipment that cleans our clothes. Not only are today's washers and dryers sensitive to the special needs of delicate or manmade fabrics, they're designed to be energy conscious, too.

The key to realizing that energy—and operating—savings is to buy a washer and dryer with flexible controls that you can adjust to suit different fabrics. When you shop, look for energy-saving options like these.
- *Variable wash cycles.*
- *Water-level controls.*
- *Separate wash and rinse water temperature controls.*
- *An automatic soak cycle.*
- *Super-fast spin speeds* that extract more water and reduce the time needed for drying.
- *Suds-saver controls* that automatically divert wash water into a storage tub where it is held for use during the next wash cycle.

Dryers—both gas and electric—typically operate by a timer; the drying cycle continues for a preset period of time (unless the door is opened). Some models also feature an electronic sensor, which monitors the moisture content of your clothes and stops the cycle at the correct dryness level. Timed-cycle dryers cost less, but electronic sensor models offer more potential for operating savings.

Gas or electric, timer- or sensor-operated, the dryer you buy should offer a variety of cycles to meet the heat requirements of various fabrics; easy-to-clean lint filters; a safety start button; and a strong magnetic door catch.

Side-by-side washers and dryers generally require 48 to 56 inches of wall space. Most are about 28 inches deep, with a 34- to 36-inch-high work surface (although rear control panels extend about 8 inches higher).

Space-saving stacking units (both portable and built-in) range from 24 to 28 inches wide and stand about 72 inches high. Special racks hold the dryer above a top- or front-loading washer.

All washers and dryers feature safety switches that interrupt the cycle when you open the door. Also insist on smooth porcelain enamel or stainless steel interiors and hard-wearing porcelain enamel exteriors.

An automatic washer requires installation on a level, sturdy floor with convenient hot and cold water and drainage connections, and its own 120-volt power outlet. Portable washers roll to the sink and hook up to the faucet. A full-size electric dryer needs its own 240-volt circuit, and must be vented to the outside. A venting distance of more than 30 feet, or many bends in the line, will cut down the dryer's efficiency. Portable dryers (all are electric) require no venting and plug into a 120-volt outlet.

UPRIGHT (OR OVER-UNDER) WASHER AND DRYER

SIDE-BY-SIDE WASHER AND DRYER

VENTILATING EQUIPMENT

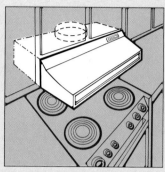

DUCTED HOOD

DUCTLESS HOOD

WALL FAN

Getting rid of food odors, fumes, and smoke is reason enough to ventilate your kitchen. But removing excess heat and moisture—especially if your home is air conditioned—also saves on the cost of energy.

Ventilation systems are sized according to the amount of air they'll move in one minute. To determine the capacity you need, measured in cubic feet per minute (CFM), multiply your kitchen square footage by two. For example, if you have a 15x20-foot kitchen, you'll need a system with a 600 CFM rating (15x20x2).

Remember that fans differ in the amount of noise they make. Check the "sone" rating on each unit you're considering; the lower the rating, the quieter the fan. Centrifugal blowers usually are quieter than propeller-type fans.

The type and placement of your range hood or fan are just as important as the CFM rating in getting the most efficient ventilation. Here are your ventilation options.

An *exhaust fan,* your least expensive choice, simply draws stale air out of the kitchen. Although not as effective as a range hood for trapping cooking odors and fumes, an exhaust fan benefits from a wall or ceiling installation as close to the range as possible.

A *vented (ducted) hood* mounted above the range has a fan that pulls stale air and cooking odors out of the kitchen and vents them to the outside. The hood should extend across the full width of the cooking area, with its bottom edge 21 to 24 inches (never more than 30 inches) above the range surface. When placed against a wall, a range hood should have a minimum capacity of 50 to 70 CFM per linear foot of range. A hood mounted over a surface unit on an island or peninsula should have at least two or three times that capacity. For

HOOD WITH WARMING LAMP

COMBINATION MICROWAVE OVEN AND RANGE HOOD

SELF-VENTING RANGE

maximum efficiency, keep ducting distance as short as possible. Too many bends or variations in duct size will allow grease to collect.

A *non-vented (ductless) hood* should be your choice only if venting to the outside is impossible. This hood contains a fan that draws air through a replaceable activated charcoal filter, which absorbs cooking odors. A second washable filter traps some cooking grease. Non-vented hoods aren't able to remove heat and humidity, however.

Self-venting ranges and cooktops don't need an overhead hood. Instead, they draw odors, grease, and moisture down into a built-in vent that's ducted to the outside.

Some range hoods do more than just vent your kitchen. You'll find models equipped with *built-in warming lamps* to keep food hot. A space-saving *combination microwave oven and range hood* gives you the convenience of an eye-level microwave oven and a range hood in the same space that a conventional 30-inch range hood alone would occupy. Choose either a ducted or ductless model.

When you shop for kitchen ventilating equipment, consider these additional features:
• A *dual-intake system* captures smoke and heat at the ceiling as well as over the range.
• A *removable filter and fan blade* facilitate periodic cleaning of grease buildup.
• A *hood or fan with a work light* adds task lighting to your rangetop.
• *Variable controls* give you a choice of fan speeds.

93

LIGHTING

Of all the components in your kitchen, lighting is the one you can least afford to skimp on. Not only can poor lighting make the cheeriest kitchen seem dreary, it can also promote fatigue and even cause accidents. A good rule of thumb: incorporate enough general, task, and accent lighting in your kitchen so that you're never working in a shadow.

You'll likely outfit your kitchen with a combination of incandescent and fluorescent bulbs. Incandescent bulbs (or lamps, as they're known to the trade) are made in a wide range of wattages, but those in the 60- to 200-watt range are your best bets for a kitchen. Bulbs typically last from 750 hours (for high-wattage bulbs) to 2,500 hours (for low-wattage and ''long life'' bulbs).

Fluorescent tubes give off between two and three times as much light per watt as incandescent bulbs, and are more economical to operate. Though the life-span of a fluorescent tube exceeds that of an incandescent bulb, it's shortened if the tube is frequently turned on and off. Choose fluorescents for your kitchen carefully; ''warm white'' tubes (rather than the harsher ''cool white'' type) are more flattering to food.

To light an average-size 10x12-foot kitchen, you'll need about 250 watts of incandescent light, or 90 watts of fluorescent light. To combine the two, allow about 2 watts of incandescent or ¾ watt of fluorescent light for every square foot of kitchen space.

Of course, your particular kitchen lighting requirements depend on a number of things —ceiling height, ceiling color, and your overall kitchen color scheme. Light, pale colors re-

A. SOFFIT CANISTER LIGHTS

B. TRACK LIGHT

C. DESK LIGHT

flect nearly twice as much light as deep, dark colors.

Your kitchen lighting options
Since most kitchen chores take place at the sink, you'll want it especially well-lighted.

D. UNDER-CABINET FLUORESCENT LIGHTS

E. DROPPED FIXTURE

F. LIGHTED RANGE VENTILATING HOOD

If your sink is under a window, opt for a recessed downlight that provides at least 150 watts of incandescent illumination, or fluorescents behind a diffuser panel. For a sink that's under a cabinet or shelf, choose diffused fluorescent tubes, or *soffit canister lights* recessed in the soffit bulkhead or upper kitchen cabinets.

Of all your kitchen lighting options, *track lights* offer the most versatility. Fixtures come in myriad styles, and give the look of built-in lighting without the installation hassle. Tracks mount on ceilings or walls, for task lighting at work centers or general kitchen illumination. For task lighting, fit track fixtures with spotlight bulbs; for general illumination, install more diffuse floodlight bulbs.

A *desk light* augments your general kitchen lighting at a kitchen office or planning center. An adjustable reading light fitted with a 50- to 75-watt incandescent bulb is adequate for all but extended reading.

Easy-to-install *under-cabinet fluorescent lights* are excellent counter-top illumination. Hide the tubes with a baffle, cornice, or diffuser panel, and let them extend at least two-thirds of the length of the counter.

If you use a *dropped fixture* over your eating area, choose one scaled in size to complement your table, and in brightness to harmonize with the rest of your kitchen. Plan on a minimum of 150 watts, but also use a dimmer switch or three-way bulb to vary the light level. Mount a dropped fixture 28 to 36 inches above the table so it doesn't obstruct the view of your diners.

Finally, a *lighted range ventilating hood,* outfitted with at least 60 watts of illumination, avoids shadows when you work at the range. For a range or cooktop not equipped with a hood, achieve the same effect with recessed downlights or soffit canisters.

CABINETS

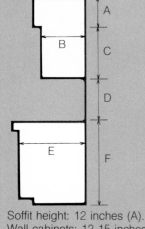

Soffit height: 12 inches (A). Wall cabinets: 12-15 inches (B), 12-33 inches (C). Base cabinets: 24 inches (E), 36 inches (F). Backsplash: 19 inches (D).

Country to contemporary—cabinets set the style of your kitchen. And here your stylistic choices are many: a single cabinet manufacturer may offer a dozen or more, in almost as many different materials.

Whichever style you choose, carefully examine the materials and construction of a sample cabinet before you buy. Here's how to tell if you're getting the quality you're paying for.

Since cabinet woods and materials come in a wide range of finishes, know what you're getting. Low-cost stock cabinets are often made of particleboard with a printed woodgrain veneer or lacquer finish. Mid- to high-priced cabinets feature selected hardwoods or soft woods that are laminated with a hardwood veneer. Prefinished birch, maple, walnut, ash, cherry, pecan, and good grades of pine are common. Metal and plastic

BASE CABINETS

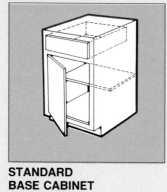

**STANDARD
BASE CABINET**

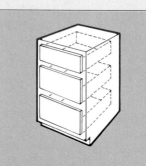

**THREE-DRAWER
BASE CABINET**

**FOUR-DRAWER
BASE CABINET**

WALL CABINETS

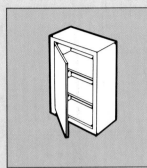

SINGLE-DOOR WALL CABINET

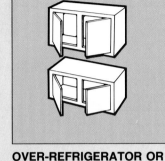

OVER-REFRIGERATOR OR -SINK WALL CABINETS

DOUBLE-DOOR WALL CABINET

PENINSULA WALL CABINET

SPECIAL CABINETS

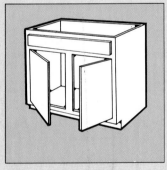

SINK BASE CABINET

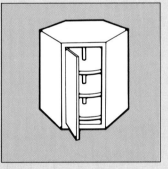

LAZY SUSAN CABINET

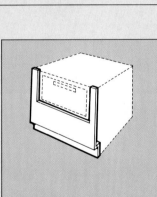

DROP-IN RANGE-FRONT CABINET

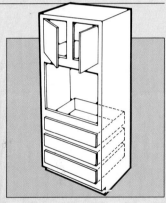

OVEN CABINET

laminated wood cabinets offer easy-care surfaces with plenty of variety in color and texture.

When you shop, look for all of these signs of quality construction: dovetail joints, ball bearing drawer glides, solidly mortised hinges, magnetic catches, heavy-duty pulls, and well-finished interiors with adjustable shelves.

Cabinet categories

There are only three broad types of kitchen cabinets: base, wall, and specialized cabinets. *Base cabinets,* which provide both storage space and a work surface, usually

measure about 24 inches deep and 34½ inches high. Adding a counter top brings them up to 36 inches—not coincidentally the height of most dishwashers, compactors, and freestanding ranges.

Base cabinets usually have one drawer at the top, but some (called base drawer units) consist entirely of drawers and are especially useful near the sink and range.

Wall cabinets, so-named because they typically mount on walls, also can hang from the ceiling over a peninsula or island. They range from 12 to 15 inches deep and 12 to 33 inches in height. Shorter 12- to 15-inch-high wall cabinets usu-

ally mount above tall refrigerators and high-oven ranges; 18-inch-high cabinets fit over standard ranges, over the sink (when there is no window), and over smaller refrigerators.

Specialized cabinets add even more convenience to meal preparation and kitchen cleanup. Just one example: diagonal corner base and wall cabinets fitted with lazy Susans turn awkward spaces into hard-working storage areas.

Under the sink, either a sink front or a sink cabinet provides storage. The sink cabinet is a complete box with a floor and back; the sink front has an optional floor but no back.

A drop-in range-front cabinet holds the range between two side rails on a base that can double as storage for large baking pans. An oven cabinet provides a central space for a slide-in oven and storage above and below.

Other popular specialized cabinets offer custom features, without custom prices. Most cabinet manufacturers sell pantries of all sizes, pull-out work surfaces, roll-out shelves, mixer/food processor centers, and microwave oven cabinets. In addition, many cabinet manufacturers are willing to modify their stock cabinets to your order for special equipment or space requirements.

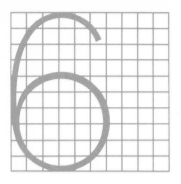

6

PUTTING IT ALL TOGETHER

You've decided what kind of kitchen your family needs. You've settled on a style, narrowed down the possible layouts, and made lists of components. Now to get down to the remodeling itself, where the wishful thinkers separate from the doers. You're ready to put it all together, to take your dreaming, thinking, and planning, and turn them into reality. This phase requires a hard nose and a sharp pencil, because you're going to start dealing with architects, designers, contractors, and bankers. Now's the time, too, when you have to decide how much of the job you're going to do yourself.

WORKING WITH AN ARCHITECT OR DESIGNER

This sleek kitchen expansion demonstrates what can happen when an architect and a pair of homeowners successfully work together. The homeowners wanted a clean, open look that would incorporate eating space and a hardworking center island. A glance at the photo of the finished result and you know immediately that the architect understood their wishes perfectly; it's hard to tell where the kitchen ends and the eating area begins. And that island provides not only a wealth of storage space, but a cooktop as well.

Another requirement was a double-decker oven arrangement (see the "after" plan, *opposite*)—one microwave and one conventional—and a planning center that would be a part of the kitchen, but not exactly in it.

The before and after plans also show how the architect did all this with an addition that accommodates the sunny breakfast room as well as a screened porch.

Getting the most from a professional
Before calling in an architect or designer, list your priorities in descending order of importance. At the top of your list, put all the things you absolutely must have; taper off with things you can live without. If there are any features you vehemently dislike in a kitchen (the owner of the one pictured here detested clutter), put those down as well. Draw some rough sketches. Clip magazine pictures of kitchens that appeal to you and turn these over to the architect, too.

In short, provide the architect or designer with every bit of helpful information you can think of. The more he knows, the better job he'll do.

Remember, too, that communication is a two-way street. When your architect or designer suggests alternatives, listen carefully. He's been through this process many times before. He knows what will work best, wear the longest, cost the least, and satisfy the most.

Be sure to discuss your plans with some idea of cost in mind. If your budget is $5,000, tell your architect or designer at the outset so he doesn't come back to you with three ways to spend $25,000.

You also should settle on what the architect's or designer's fee will include. Will he just turn over the finished drawings and disappear, or will he supervise construction and stay with the job until the last coat of paint goes on? Agree on how he will charge you for his services: by the hour or the day, with a flat fee, or as a percentage of the total construction cost. Get everything straight in the beginning —and in writing—and you'll have much less chance of expensive misunderstandings or regrets later.

How to find a good architect or designer
The ones who do the best work will generally benefit from word-of-mouth advertising, so ask around. Then look at finished jobs the architects or designers have done. If you're still stymied, call up the local chapters of the American Institute of Architects or the American Institute of Building Designers. If you're working with kitchen designers, look for the initials NKBA, which indicate membership in the National Kitchen and Bath Association. None of these recommendations or affiliations is a guarantee of competence, but each is helpful if you have to start from scratch.

BEFORE   AFTER

KITCHEN
12 x13

DW
C   KITCHEN
12 x13
R
BREAKFAST
10 x11
OVENS   DESK

WORKING WITH A CONTRACTOR

If you're ever going to hire a contractor, a kitchen remodeling offers a prime opportunity. Any remodeling can be tricky, but kitchens present problems and challenges all their own. With a contractor on your team, you'll handle most of them with ease. But first you have to know how to handle the contractor.

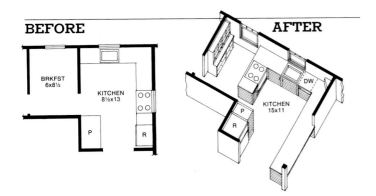

BEFORE   AFTER

A savvy contractor can make a kitchen remodeling succeed in ways you might not expect. In the project you see here, for example, you might assume that the contractor lined the walls with expensive cedar cabinetry. But no, he merely faced existing cabinets with inexpensive cedar strips.

Look at the before and after floor plans and you'll see that the contractor also took care of a couple of larger matters. He enclosed a porch and opened up the back wall to accommodate a new dining area and breakfast bar; and he tore out a partition between the old breakfast nook and the kitchen to install a peninsula, complete with drop-in range. The overall result is a handsome, functional kitchen that effectively combines jobs both large and small.

Working successfully with your contractor means communicating successfully, especially if you've bypassed the architect or designer. If you *are* using, say, an architect, the burden of communication falls primarily on him—that is, unless you release him from further responsibility after approving his working drawings. But even if the architect is overseeing the job, he won't be there more than once a day. You, on the other hand, will often be bumping into the results of the contractor's work. If you see something that looks wrong, bring it to the contractor's attention at once and get it straightened out then and there. Here are the key stages in establishing good communications.

Specifications
Make sure that your specifications contain every last detail that will affect the job—from hardware and appliances to

finishes and flooring. The more descriptive information you can incorporate, the better chance you stand of getting exactly the kitchen you want. Specify everything from grades of lumber to catalog and model numbers of appliances. This is important for two reasons: it ensures that each contractor bases his bid on exactly the same job, and it leaves no room for guesswork or finagling once the winning contractor gets the actual job under way.

The contract
Be sure it spells out everything the contractor is responsible for, even seemingly obvious tasks, such as supervision and responsibility for the work of subcontractors. Also, include the length of the contractor's guarantee, the necessity of quality workmanship, and starting and completion dates.

On those last two points: the contract should state explicitly that all elements of the job must be completed *in a workmanlike manner.* Starting and completion dates should be followed by the phrase *time is of the essence.*

Be sure to cover the schedule of payments in the contract. A commonly accepted arrangement calls for one-third of the total fee when the contract is signed, another third when the work is substantially complete, and the last third when the job is completely finished to your satisfaction.

Changes
Often, either you or the contractor will discover after the job is under way that a change not covered in either the contract or the specs would be advantageous. No problem—but, as in setting up the original contract, protect yourself by getting the change down *in writing,* including the cost.

101

DOING ALL
OR PARTS OF THE WORK
YOURSELF

If you're a dedicated do-it-yourselfer—with skills in plumbing, wiring, carpentry, and finish work—you could conceivably pull off a kitchen remodeling without spending a penny for labor. But before you don overalls, consider what your time, energy, and leisure are worth—and what several months of dust and disruption might do to your family's everyday routine. Of course, taking on work yourself needn't be an all-or-nothing proposition. Here's how to evaluate which jobs you might be willing and able to tackle yourself, and which you should delegate to a contractor or subcontractors.

The bright, contemporary kitchen shown here resulted from a collaboration between a contractor and the architect-owner. In planning a whole-house remodeling for this older two-story, the architect left the kitchen where it was, but extended it with an addition that includes an 8½x11-foot breakfast room on the ground floor, and a new study above.

With plans in hand, the contractor framed the exterior shell, then installed roofing, windows, siding, and other elements of the shell. The owner put up sheathing himself, and did all the interior work. Because the kitchen stayed where it was, he didn't have to concern himself with a lot of new plumbing and major electrical work.

Could you do the same? Maybe, but first sit down and make a dispassionate inventory of your talents. If they aren't up to the task, you could end up with a botched remodeling that's worse than none at all. What's more, mistakes in structural, plumbing, or wiring work could pose serious dangers later on.

Preparing for an all-out project

If you do decide to remodel your own kitchen with little or no professional assistance,

think through every stage of the job well in advance. Develop an accurate and detailed plan, as explained in Chapter 4. Make lists of all the materials and components you'll need (see Chapters 3 and 5). Establish a timetable that leaves room for unexpected delays or problems, and recruit helpers for heavy or difficult jobs, such as drywalling and moving appliances.

Besides the work itself, you also have to plan how your family will get along while the kitchen is out of commission. The family of the architect who designed and remodeled the kitchen shown here lived for four months without running water on the first floor. They cooked meals in a toaster oven or out on the barbecue grill. To minimize problems, consider scheduling the worst phase of your remodeling for a time when the children will be at summer camp or visiting grandparents.

Limiting your involvement

Generally, the jobs a homeowner can do most successfully are those that fall at the beginning and end of a kitchen remodeling project. At the outset you're faced with all the preparatory steps that don't demand specialized skills. You may have to remove non-load-

bearing walls; take out cabinets, fixtures, and appliances; or remove wallpaper, paint, and flooring. All of these tasks are dirty and disagreeable, but just about anyone with energy can do them.

At the other end of the job, you can lay tile, install fixtures, hang paper, and paint walls, ceilings, or cabinets. Here again, time and patience count more than expertise.

Design to suit your skills

Regardless of the extent to which you decide to participate in a remodeling, realize that lots of problems will have more than one solution—and that you can skew your planning approach toward jobs you're confident you can pull off. In the remodeling shown here, for example, a badly deteriorated ceiling in the original kitchen would have required tricky plastering or drywalling. The owner elected to simply cover it up with a series of polished metal strips.

Finally, if you do decide to try your hand at plumbing, wiring, or structural work, check with your local building department first. In some communities, codes specify that professionals must do the work, or that amateur jobs be inspected and ''signed off'' by a licensed contractor.

BEFORE   **AFTER**

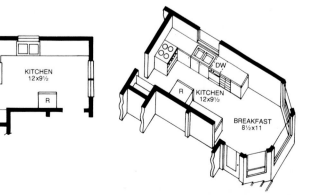

FINANCING A KITCHEN REMODELING

After you've developed a plan for your new kitchen and decided who's going to do the work, you need to face one more big question: how will you pay for it all?

If you have the cash on hand, count yourself fortunate. It costs money to borrow money, and in recent years interest rates have been running higher than ever. Availability of loans has sometimes been a problem, too.

These difficulties make it imperative that you shop as carefully for financing as you do for any of the components of your new kitchen. Here's a rundown of the major sources for remodeling money, also summarized in the table on the opposite page.

(Caution: lending laws and practices are changing rapidly, and also vary from state to state. Use our survey only as a general guide.)

Life insurance

Every "straight" or "whole" life insurance policy builds up a substantial cash value over the years, and you may borrow against it any time you like. When interest rates are high, this is by far your cheapest source of funds. Some newer policies have sliding rates; with many the maximum interest you'll pay is 8 percent. If your policy dates back to the '50s, '60s, or early '70s, you'll pay even less—maybe as little as 5 or 6 percent. What's more, there's no hassle. You simply call or write your agent or company for a loan application, then sign it and mail it back. In a few weeks you have your money. It's important to understand, however, that your insurance coverage will be reduced by the amount you owe.

Retirement trusts

Employer contributions to certain retirement funds, profit-sharing trusts, and savings and investment plans may sometimes be used as collateral for a loan from the trust once the funds have become vested, i.e., when you fully own them, usually after five to ten years.

Check with your company's employee benefits manager. If you qualify, you may be able to obtain the loan at lower than prevailing interest rates.

Home equity

Your home may have doubled or even tripled in value since the day you bought it. As a result, it represents an equity "windfall"—and your biggest potential source of cash, usually through a second mortgage. Second mortgages can be expensive, though—2 to 5 percentage points or more above the going mortgage rates. Also, you might have to repay the loan sooner than you'd like. Fifteen years is about tops; five years is not uncommon. That means you could face some hefty monthly payments on top of your existing mortgage payments.

Before you go for a second mortgage, review your first mortgage to see if refinancing might make more sense. If it dates back 15 years or more, it could contain a clause that lets you reopen the mortgage at the old interest rate. And even if it doesn't, your lending institution might be willing to give you a break of some kind just to get your low-interest mortgage off its books. That could mean any number of things—from a couple of percentage points off to forgiveness of a portion of the indebtedness. A relatively new wrinkle is a "blended" combination of your old rate and the current rate. Be sure to ask about these possibilities—and don't be afraid to negotiate.

Refinancing makes even more sense if your old mortgage is held by the Federal National Mortgage Association. Fannie Mae, as it's called, holds both FHA and VA mortgages in its portfolio, as well as a considerable number of conventional mortgages. If yours is among them (you'll probably have to check with your lender to find out), you can borrow up to 90 percent of your home's current market value at a fixed rate that's often as much as 2 or 3 percentage points below the current market rate for new mortgages. The term is 30 years unless you want it shorter. Other sources for a second mortgage include:

• *Credit unions* typically charge less interest than other lenders, as much as a full percentage point below current first mortgage rates.

• *Savings and loan associations* are increasingly writing second mortgages, and normally at comparatively low rates—usually 2 or more percentage points above current first-mortgage rates. Durations run from three to 20 years; maximum allowable indebtedness depends on whether you deal with a federal- or state-chartered S & L.

• *Commercial banks* are not likely to let you have a second mortgage unless you're already a customer, though your previous business need not include your first mortgage. You can borrow up to 90 percent at a national bank, and 80 percent at a state bank. Terms run up to 15 years, but the mortgage is subject to review every three years. At this point, one of two things could happen: the mortgage might be "rolled over" (rewritten) at a new rate to reflect the current cost of money—generally at 1 or 2 points above the going prime rate; or the bank could "call" the loan. In the latter case, you'll be required to make a "balloon" payment and pay off the balance all at once.

• *Mutual savings banks* are generally permitted to issue mortgages up to 80 percent of total indebtedness on market value. Terms extend up to 15 years, but are "callable" for renegotiation after three years. Rates are typically 2 or more percentage points above those charged on first mortgages.

• *Consumer finance companies* lend up to 90 percent on current value, with most loans written on an installment basis for ten years. Rates vary greatly depending on state laws (see chart).

Stocks and bonds

With the exception of savings and loans, all the sources mentioned above also will make loans against negotiable securities. So will most stockbrokers. Normally you can borrow up to 50 percent of a stock's market value, more on bonds. The interest rate is about the same as on second mortgages.

Savings accounts

You can borrow against any type of savings. Rates tend to be only a point or two above the interest you collect on your account. Of course, you have to decide whether you'd be better off to simply cash in the account and pay for your new kitchen outright.

SOURCES FOR REMODELING MONEY

	ADVANTAGES	DISADVANTAGES	SPECIAL NOTES
LIFE INSURANCE	No red tape. Lowest interest rates. You select the term. In essence, you're borrowing your own money, yet your policy remains in effect. You pay interest on the loan, but you can pay back the principal whenever you choose.	Face value reduced by amount of loan, plus interest, in the event of your death.	You can lapse-proof your policy by leaving enough cash value on deposit to cover your next premium. Some policies carry an option allowing you to keep the full benefit intact by using your annual dividends to buy renewable term life insurance in the amount of your loan indebtedness.
RETIREMENT TRUSTS	Probability of low rates. Interest payments augment your share of the fund and remain tax-sheltered until withdrawal. Interest is tax-deductible.	Borrowed portion of trust does not appreciate in value while you are using it.	Whether you can borrow from a trust depends on how your company's fund was set up.
HOME EQUITY	A second mortgage leaves the first mortgage undisturbed, costs less up front than a first mortgage, usually involves no prepayment penalty. Refinancing creates opportunity to negotiate a lower than going rate.	Second mortgages carry high rates of interest and specify short repayment periods. A new mortgage will also carry a high rate of interest—as well as substantial new closing costs. Credit unions may limit the amount you can borrow to $10,000 or $20,000. State-chartered S & Ls normally set a limit of 80 percent. Rates at consumer finance companies can go well above prime, and often do.	Second mortgages are legal in most states. Refinancing also is legal in most states, but is usually unwise when you have an existing mortgage at a low rate—unless you can negotiate a lower than going rate with the lender. Rates at consumer finance companies vary widely, depending on state laws and the availability of money.
STOCKS AND BONDS	Available from most lending institutions (except S & Ls) as well as from stockbrokers.	If value of the stock declines, you could be "called for margin"—that is, required to put up additional funds.	Highly volatile stocks tend not to impress lenders favorably.
SAVINGS ACCOUNTS	Low rates.	Penalties for early withdrawal could easily cancel any cost advantages.	If you have savings, you may decide to cash them in rather than borrow against them.

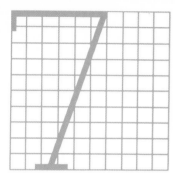

WHAT ELSE COULD YOUR KITCHEN DO?

No one in a family plays just one role anymore. A mother is also a member of the work force, Dad is the weekend chef, and kids are everything from star quarterbacks to bookworms or ballerinas.

In a society like ours, it's ridiculous to think any room in our homes is going to get by performing just one function. So today's kitchens are expanding their horizons. They're also family rooms, craft quarters, greenhouses, wine cellars, party places—even computer centers. Whatever else you'd like your kitchen to do, this chapter shows you how to do it.

Kitchens are opening up and including adjacent areas for a revival of the old "keeping room," that cozy spot in a house where the whole family assembles to talk, create a project, or just relax. Of course, family dining—even entertaining—remains a function of this newfound social area, as in the kitchen/keeping room shown here.

Invade outer space

To create your family kitchen, you must have or acquire the necessary space. If you've got kitchen cramps, look to surrounding areas such as a porch, utility room, or pantry; or maybe a little-used formal dining room would be more functional as a family activity area. (To annex adjacent space, see pages 66 and 67.)

When you've got a bead on your outer space, visualize the entire area as one large room, sans dividing walls. Then start to plan your space so it works most efficiently.

Activities first

If yours is a reading, relaxing, or TV-viewing family, you'll want plenty of comfortable seating in your family area. If, instead, you're puzzle workers, homeworkers, crafters, or project people, you'll need both work and storage space.

In the kitchen, take the same kind of activity inventory. Do you do a lot of baking, entertaining, or canning? Is food preparation a team effort?

The family whose kitchen is shown here has opted for features to aid entertaining. When the wall was removed between the kitchen and the old pantry and maid's room, the new kitchen featured more storage, more serving space, and additional appliances, geared for large-scale food service.

(continued)

FAMILY
KITCHENS

(continued)

Use, not size, is the hall-mark of a successful family kitchen. Using a room and enjoying it depend on practicalities such as floor plans, traffic patterns, furnishings, lighting, and surfaces that don't require a building maintenance crew to keep looking good. Here are the main points to consider.

In laying out your family kitchen, few things are as important as the traffic pattern you establish. Though you want to retain the openness and friendliness of this multi-function area, you still must keep the mainstream of traffic out of your kitchen work areas.

To accomplish this, first provide access to the family room through some area other than the kitchen.

Next, define your kitchen area with low dividers. The combination kitchen shown here directs traffic effectively by enclosing the cook center in a peninsula divider. The chef can enjoy the family room's fun without a parade of people through the kitchen's business district.

If islands or dividers, such as peninsula counters, servers, or sideboards, are not available, direct traffic by rearranging your furniture. Backs of chairs or sofas, floor-standing plants, or tables can form inconspicuous "corridors" that direct pedestrian traffic.

Your room in a new light

When you're planning activities, be sure you consider light. Your kitchen needs general light, but it also needs specialized lighting in work areas. This also holds true in your family room. You'll want soft, low-level lighting for relaxing or TV, brighter general lighting for family meals or game playing, and, very possibly, some specialized lighting for doing homework or projects. Some helpers for this kind of versatile lighting are ceiling track lights, under-cabinet light fixtures, and dimmer switches on overhead lights.

When it comes to the surface

Never lose sight of the fact that your kitchen/family room will be a hard-working and -playing area with heavy use. Plan your materials accordingly. Make sure furniture upholstery is stain-repellent, use only easy-care floor coverings throughout the two activity areas, and take care that table tops are laminated plastic or coated with polyurethane. You'll save yourself work and replacement costs by investing at the outset in heavy-duty, easy-to-maintain surfaces.

The kitchen/family room shown here has ceramic tile in a graphic diagonal design all around the lower portion of the walls. The same tile is used to surface the kitchen, making cleanup a breeze.

The ties that bind

Even though you've worked hard to create two inter-functioning areas, you still want the space to look like a single room. The best way to accomplish this is to keep the two areas compatible in style and feeling. Carry floor, ceiling, and wall coverings from one activity center to the other. Let the same colors flow from kitchen to family room, and tie the areas together with fabric, using similar patterns for window treatments, chair cushions, place mats, napkins, and even upholstery.

Furnishing for fun

A potentially comfortable and inviting family room might, instead, be a put-off if the furniture isn't casual and comfortable. Save formal furnishings and elegant fabrics for another room. Let this one be what the family wants—a place to take shoes off and relax without being afraid of dirtying the damask.

Culinary arts now share floor space with traditional arts and crafts, which are nestling in beside them in today's expanded kitchens. Crafting close to kitchen activities means you're no longer isolated in a single-person pursuit. You're with the family —where the fun is!

If your creativity goes beyond cooking, you're a prime candidate for a kitchen craft center. And, depending on your craft, of course, there's bound to be a way to put your two interests together.

Whatever your pursuit, it will require some amount of work space, space to store equipment or supplies, and good lighting. Those are the general needs. We'll look at them first, then go on to some specifics.

Left out
Your mother may have taught you to pick up your toys, but there are just times when picking up your craft equipment is not only impossible, it's also unnecessary.

If your interest involves a large item such as a loom, quilting frame, needlework frame, or easel, leave it in the open. Select and arrange the furniture of your room to accommodate it, just as the weaver shown *opposite* has done. Here, a small loom is very much a part of the furnishings in this adjacent-to-the-kitchen craft center, and the weaver's careful planning has left her ample room for working, as well.

There's no need to hide your craft materials either. Used as interesting accents, colorful hanks of yarn or bolts of fabric become integral to a room's decorative scheme. A wall-mounted shelf or cubbyhole unit will keep supplies neat and organized, yet show off their bright colors or interesting textures to advantage.

On the other hand, if your craft equipment and materials are better off tucked away, try engineering a wall-mounted, fold-down work and storage unit à la Mr. Murphy's bed. Or invest in a dual-purpose piece of furniture that lets you pull a work table out of a cabinet and shut it away from view when you're through working.

Light is necessary in work or craft areas. Plan the intensity and amount of light according to the detail required by your craft; try a floor lamp or wall-mounted draftsman's lamp.

Other considerations
Now let's look at some other crafty things to consider:

• Power outlets near your work area if your craft calls for electrical tools or accessories.
• Easy-to-clean surfaces on walls and floor if your craft tends to be messy.
• A sink or close proximity to the kitchen sink if your craft requires water or water cleanup.
• Counter space or folding tables for family snacks if your craft temporarily occupies the dining table.
• Wall or shelf space on which to display your craft items. The whole cooking and eating area takes on the character of your craft when you adopt finished products as one-of-a-kind accessories for your kitchen craft center, as shown *below*.

LAUNDRY CENTERS

No two household chores occur with more regularity than meal preparation and laundry. For that reason, it makes great sense to put the two functions as close to one another as possible. In a day when conservation of both time and energy is a consideration, why waste either by running between a kitchen in one area of the house and a laundry center in another?

Once you've decided to relocate your laundry closer to—or into—the kitchen, your first step is the space search. Some logical places to look include the end wall of your kitchen, or adjacent areas such as a pantry or breakfast nook.

How much space do you need?

Though an efficient laundry center includes more than just a washer and dryer, those two appliances are the imperatives, so plan your space around them. And don't be fooled. All washers and dryers are not the same size.

A pair of full-size (not compact) appliances, side by side, requires from 48 to 56 inches of wall space. A stacked arrangement (providing your units are stackable) occupies from 24 to 28 inches in width and about 72 inches in height.

Other essentials

Your kitchen laundry area will also require the following:
• Water connection. Luckily, proximity to the kitchen will mean plumbing is nearby.
• Drain for the washer.
• Electrical outlet (if your dryer is electric, you will need a 220-volt circuit).
• Gas connection if your dryer is not an electric model.
• Venting for the dryer. The most effective venting is to the outside. If your laundry center is located on an inside wall, it may be advisable to vent the dryer down through the floor, then through a crawl space or the basement to the outside.

More function factors

For a fully functioning laundry center, consider adding these:

• Cabinet space. You'll want to store laundry products close to appliances. If you have small children, make sure the laundry product cabinet is either locked or up out of reach.
• Counter space for folding clothes. (In a pinch, the top surfaces of side-by-side appliances can serve this purpose.)
• Counter-top and floor-covering materials that are impervious to water, detergent, and bleach.
• A wall outlet for an iron or a hand steamer.
• Storage area for an iron, ironing supplies, and a variety of mending materials.

• Hanging space for clothes as they come from the dryer. This might be nothing more than a wall-mounted, fold-back rack or a slide-out unit mounted inside a top cabinet.
• A pretreating sink is a handy addition to a full-scale laundry area. But if your kitchen sink is already nearby, you may not feel a need for this option.

Hide it all

You may want your laundry area to be your own well-kept secret. In that case, there are several ways to mask the area completely when not in use.

The laundry room on this page features white appliances simply tucked into a kitchen alcove; the laundry *opposite* has gone to great lengths to make the washday area look like the rest of the kitchen—even to enclosing the appliances in cabinets, with a lift-up section in the counter top for access to the top-loading washer.

Other quicker cover-ups include fronting your laundry center with bifold doors, a Roman shade, or a roll-down wood-slat shade.

COMPUTER AND PLANNING CENTERS

Home computers are no longer a fantasy out of science fiction—they're here and they're hard at work doing a long list of home management chores. You can just bring one home, wire a few components together, plug the unit in, and use it. Or you can plan a complete kitchen computer center that not only incorporates a variety of home-office activities, but also allows for growth as you discover even more applications. Either way, we'll give you some tips on how to go about putting a personal computer on your kitchen staff.

Home computers are now more economically priced and easier to use than ever before. You don't need to be a tycoon or an engineer to put one to use—and once you know what it can do, you'll wonder how you got along without it.

With a home computer you've got electronic help doing the family taxes, balancing your checkbook, keeping the household budget in check, monitoring energy usage, and reminding you of upcoming appointments.

In kitchen management, your computer can help you with diet and menu planning, food inventory, shopping lists, storing and displaying recipes, food values and data—it can even activate individual appliances. And besides all this, it can function as a learning and entertainment center for the whole family.

Computer facts

Generally, home computer systems are composed of three units: a TV-like monitor (could even be your TV), a keyboard similar to an electric typewriter's, and a portable cassette tape recorder or shoe-box-size box with slots in the face. (This third unit handles ''software''—either tapes or discs that store information.) Prices depend on what your system includes.

Where to install it

If you're putting in a kitchen computer/office center, look for a place that's convenient to other kitchen activities, but removed enough so that you have some elbow room for working.

On this page is a home office/computer center in a free-standing divider unit, all within a kitchen. The kitchen *opposite* makes use of a cantilevered shelf for its computer's home base.

Potential office spaces in and around your kitchen might include an end wall, an alcove, the end of a counter in a corner of your kitchen, or a closet that's ventilated. Nearly any small spot can be made to work well if you can incorporate these essentials:

• A sturdy, non-vibrating table. The computer weighs in at about 35 pounds and should be firmly supported.

• Enough table and counter space around the computer to accommodate papers or books.

• A 110-volt power outlet. Though your computer doesn't draw a great deal of power, it is affected by ''surging,'' so avoid using it on a circuit with motor-driven appliances.

• A desk or kitchen chair.

Some of the extras that can make your computer center more versatile include bookshelves, files, drawer or storage space for office supplies, and a telephone.

Some safeguards

Your home computer is a sensitive piece of electronic equipment. Though it needs no special pampering, it will do better if left in one place, rather than being jostled from spot to spot.

Avoid extreme heat. Keep your computer a safe distance from heat registers, heat-producing appliances such as ranges or ovens, or heat- and moisture-producing appliances such as dishwashers.

114

WINE STORAGE
AND
WET BARS

Every party is the same! All the guests tend to congregate in the kitchen, mostly around the refrigerator or sink. Paradoxically, home entertaining that's less formal in dress and decor is becoming more formal in substance—in food and drink. Now add to gourmet cooking the fact that America is fast becoming a nation of wine aficionados. Look at your kitchen in light of these two factors; there may never be a better time to expand its functions with wine storage, and for more traditional tastes, a wet bar.

With more and more Americans enjoying wine, many more American kitchens are incorporating some sort of wine storage. But remember, storing wine isn't simply a matter of stashing the bottles any which way—or anywhere that's handy. A good bottle of wine has to be stored properly in order to realize its full potential.

To provide the best storage possible, you have to understand the elemental characteristics of wine.

Heat and light destroy a wine's quality. Store wine in a dark, cool place (55 to 60 degrees Fahrenheit is ideal, though in a kitchen, certainly not usual). Plan your kitchen wine storage area away from heat-producing appliances such as ranges, ovens, dishwashers, or even refrigerators. Avoid heating pipes or radiators, and don't locate your wine storage area where sunlight and heat will hit it.

Realize, too, that while it makes sense to keep handy wines you'll use in the next few weeks, a kitchen is not the best place for vintages you'd like to age a year or two. These do best in a cool location, such as a basement or attached garage, where the bottles won't be disturbed.

How to store wine
The best way to store a wine bottle is on its side. This position keeps the cork from drying out, which prevents air from entering the bottle and spoiling the wine.

A variety of ready-made wine racks is available; adding a wine storage area to your kitchen may be as simple as bringing one of these home, finding a good spot for it, and setting it up. The kitchen *below* utilizes space between top and base cabinets for a handsome wood wine rack. The kitchen *opposite*, *right*, contains a section of cabinet equipped with shelves for bottle storage and a shelf/rack arrangement for glass storage. In the other kitchen wet bar on the same page, wine is stored in a bottom drawer, near the floor

where the room's temperature is coolest.

The bar exam

Adding a wet bar to your kitchen is a good way to make the area more operational as well as the social center of every party. To create a kitchen bar, consider any or all of these options:

• *Sink.* You'll need a plumbing hookup and counter space to accommodate the sink. Hospitality sinks range in size from 15 inches square to 15x25 inches. A welcome option is a lined well for bottles. Some sinks come with faucets, others don't. If you're buying your own, your best choice is either an 8- or 10-inch gooseneck faucet.

• *Refrigerator.* An under-counter refrigerator is a convenient addition to your bar. It will require a power outlet and a space 17 to 18½ inches wide. Some compact refrigerators are square and can be built into a base cabinet unit; others are counter-top height with laminated tops that give a built-in look.

• *Storage.* Consider the things you use and plan space to house them.

Glasses may be stored on shelves, in cabinets, or hung from racks. If you're moderately handy, you can make your own racks to store stemmed glasses, or you can purchase racks and install them on the underside of shelves or wall cabinets.

Beverage storage will require a closed-door cabinet. Depending on family security measures, you may want to provide a lock for your liquor cabinet.

Bar accessories such as mixing, stirring, and muddling tools, an ice bucket, and any other miscellany will require storage in drawers or cabinets.

Appliances such as a blender, mixer, or ice crusher require additional storage space.

• *Work space.* You'll need a couple feet of counter space for preparing refreshments.

• *Light.* If your bar is built into a closet, alcove, or cabinet recess, you'll need an overhead or under-cabinet light to make the spot a cheery and well-lit work area.

• *Cover-up.* Tuck your wet bar discreetly behind bifold doors and it can disappear when the party's over.

WHAT ELSE COULD YOUR KITCHEN DO?

BUMPING OUT WITH A GREENHOUSE

At one time about all a kitchen greenhouse offered was a place to putter with a few houseplants or experiment with some exotic flora. Today's greenhouses do that, too. But they can also serve in other ways. Consider, for example, how an indoor garden could put fresh vegetables on the table year round—or how the sun's warmth could help heat adjacent areas and reduce heating costs.

When a kitchen greenhouse can help you cut both fuel and food bills, it's an investment worth considering. Many prefab units can be installed in existing windows, or as replacements for kitchen walls.

The fresh-as-all-outdoors kitchen shown here was remodeled to accommodate a 7x16-foot prefab greenhouse; its curved-glass covering rises up 10 feet. Adjustable glass shelves were added for extra storage, and aluminum shades installed for interior light and heat control.

Solar energy assist

If you're planning your kitchen greenhouse as a passive solar unit, keep these things in mind:
• Locate your greenhouse on the south side of your house to take advantage of winter sun. Its best position is due south, but 15 degrees or so east or west won't be critical.
• Avoid obstructions such as trees, hills, or other houses.
• Check your local weather bureau for weather patterns in your area. You may want to adjust the greenhouse's location a little to take extra advantage of either morning or afternoon sunshine.
• Determine the ideal angle for the greenhouse's collector, its sloped roof. A rule of thumb is to add 20 degrees to the site's latitude.
• A passive solar unit needs some sort of thermal mass to soak up heat during the day and release it during the night. A cement, brick, stone, or gravel floor works well.
• You'll need a system to control the rate at which your greenhouse gains or loses heat. When the greenhouse is an integral part of a room's interior, you'll need insulated

shades or some other device to minimize nighttime heat loss and summer overheating.

The kitchen greenhouse shown here features, in addition to its aluminum shades, peak ventilating louvers to create the good air circulation plants depend on.

How do your vegetables grow?

When your green thumb has outgrown basic houseplants, you're ready for a bumper crop of fresh vegetables from your greenhouse. Almost anything that will grow outside will thrive under glass.

There are, however, some factors a greenhouse gardener has to consider. Ventilation, soil, water, and humidity all require careful management. Here are some tips:
• Schedule watering for morning so plants can dry off before nightfall, and the onset of cooler temperatures.
• On bright, sunny days, the loss of water through evaporation is greater than on cloudy days, so water generously on bright days and hold back on dark ones.
• Coarse, sandy soil doesn't retain water as well as humus-rich soil, so you may have to water pots of sandy soil more often.
• Don't waterlog plants. Too much water will kill a plant faster than too little.
• During winter, don't use cold water directly from the tap.
• Plastic pots retain water better than porous clay pots.
• To hold down the chance of disease, soak the soil instead of watering from above through the leaves.

GROWING HERBS AND VEGETABLES IN A KITCHEN GARDEN

When you garden in a greenhouse, you can't blame a crop failure on the weather. You've moved Mother Nature out of the driver's seat, so now it's up to you to maintain healthy plants, starting with soil, seeds, moisture, and temperature levels in your kitchen greenhouse.

If you expect good crops, start with good soil. Since container soil dries out faster than outdoor garden soil, mix it to retain as much water as possible. A combination of one part peat moss to one part sand or perlite or vermiculite with some well-rotted compost helps prevent drying out and compaction. With a yard full of earth, it may seem silly to buy commercial soil. There are some distinct advantages, but the decision is yours.

If you use garden loam, mix it with equal parts of peat moss and coarse sand. If your garden soil is already on the sandy side, eliminate addition of the extra sand.

Commercial mixes are sterile—free from soil-borne diseases. They're also packed with the nutrients essential to good plant growth. You can sterilize your own soil, but it's messy and time-consuming. If you're willing to spend a little on commercial soil, you're ensured of giving your greenhouse crops a good start.

Or grow vegetables hydroponically—without soil. Rather than being set in soil, plants grow from an artificial aggregate such as perlite, vermiculite, coarse sand, or gravel. Watering with a special solution provides all the nutrients necessary for plant growth.

Going to pot?

Pot gardening requires containers that have adequate drainage to keep vegetables' roots from rotting. Poke holes in plastic pots with a screwdriver or ice pick if necessary. Clay pots usually have drainage holes when you buy them.

Your pots should be large enough to hold a normal root system. Undersized pots can turn foliage yellow for lack of nutrients.

Large vegetables, such as tomatoes and zucchini, need plastic tubs at least 12 inches deep. Smaller crops, such as carrots, radishes, and herbs, can get by with 9-inch depths.

Feeding time in the greenhouse

Unless you're growing vegetables hydroponically, your plants need added food from time to time. Several types of fertilizers serve this purpose.

Dry fertilizer is usually mixed with the growing medium. Wet fertilizer is diluted with water and applied to the soil with a watering can. ''Slow release'' fertilizers are valuable because they provide nutrients a little at a time.

Keep in mind that too much fertilizer is worse than too little. If over-applied, it can burn roots and stems, or result in plants that produce all leaves and no vegetables or fruit. Some other pointers:
• Make sure soil is moist before applying fertilizer, to avoid burning roots.
• Mix fertilizer half-strength for plants that demand less food, such as most herbs.
• Avoid salt buildups—whitish deposits on soil and pot rims. As a cure, ''leach'' by drenching the soil with tepid water until the excess runs out the bottom of the pot.

Villains, special needs

Insects and lack of humidity are both dangers to your plants. Humidity levels should be between 50 and 70 percent. Keep plants misted for best results.

To keep bugs in check, remove all dead leaves and give plants plenty of growing room to prevent overcrowding and poor ventilation.

Different vegetables require different growing conditions, different care, and different harvesting procedures. The chart *at right* tells about nine favorites.

VEGETABLES FOR GREENHOUSE GARDENS

VEGETABLE	VARIETIES	PLANTING	CARE	HARVEST
Beans	Bush Beans (Tendercrop and Greensleeves; Cherokee and Gold Crop in yellow beans)	Start from seeds. Adapts to a wide variety of soil types.	Likes warm temperatures. Fertilize when plants are 4 to 6 inches high.	Pick when young and tender.
Carrots	Royal Chantenay or Scarlet Nantes best for shallow soil	Start from seeds. Plant ½ inch deep. Grows well in a soil/peat moss mix.	Likes cool temperatures. After they have sprouted, thin to one every 3 inches.	Yield in 70-120 days. Pick when tops of roots are about ½ inch in diameter.
Chard	Red (Rhubarb Chard) and green (Lucullus and Fordhook Giant)	Start from seeds. Prefers alkaline soil.	Likes cool temperatures; otherwise not finicky.	Ready in 60 days. Pick outer leaves as they mature.
Cucumber	Bush type (Pot Luck and Bush Whopper)	Start from seeds. Needs plenty of water, well-drained soil.	Likes warm soil (above 60° F.), high humidity. Train plants to climb a trellis. Thin to 4 inches apart.	Ready in about 60 days. Pick when small and green.
Eggplant	Black Beauty particularly good large-fruit variety for pots	Buy nursery plants. Water generously.	Likes warm air and regular fertilizing. Space 12 inches apart.	Ready in about 70 days. Remove fruit with pruning shears.
Lettuce	Leaf and loose head types	Start from seeds. Cover with no more than ¼ inch of soil. Sprinkle with water.	Prefers cool temperatures and moist humus soils.	Ready in 8-12 weeks. Pick outer leaves first (leaf types). Pull head lettuce only after entire plant matures.
Peppers	Sweet (Tokyo Bell and Bell Boy). Hot (Long Red Cayenne and Hot Portugal)	Start with nursery plants. Soil needs good drainage.	Prefers medium to warm temperatures.	Ready in about 50 days. Pick when peppers are the desired size.
Radishes	Cherry Belle, White Icicle, and Sparkler	Start from seeds. Sow every two weeks to replenish crop.	Likes cool temperatures. Thin plants to 1 inch apart.	Ready in 3 to 4 weeks. Pick when root tops protrude through soil.
Tomatoes	Pixies, Tiny Tim, or patio varieties	Buy nursery plants. Use properly fertilized soil and not too much nitrogen.	Needs warm temperatures. Stake plants. Cherry types are fine in hanging planters and will set fruit as long as temperature is above 50° F. Container size for cherry tomatoes should equal 1 gallon.	Ready in 52 to 70 days. Tomatoes are ready when they pull easily from the vines.

8

STOCKING YOUR KITCHEN

When you fill your kitchen shelves, shop for quality. A good tool rewards you with years of trouble-free use, and better-quality foodstuffs make for better-tasting recipes. The next few pages show the basic equipment and supplies you might need to set up a kitchen. Make your choices according to how you cook. Besides quality, consider durability, safety, storage, and ease of cleaning. Whenever possible, opt for tools that perform multiple functions, and staples that make a variety of dishes.

1 Tea infuser, candy thermometer, rolling pin, grater, timer, vegetable peeler, measuring cup, cookie cutters, sifter, pastry blender

2 Meat pounder, ice pick, slotted spoon, perforated turner, colander, ice cream scoop, can opener

3 (Top row) corkscrew, tongs, natural-bristle pastry brush, measuring cups (dry), apple corer/slicer, nested measuring spoons, whisk, kitchen shears

4 Utility fork, ladle, nutcracker, whisk, cheese slicer, garlic press, butcher knife, grapefruit knife, spatula, boner, slicer, utility knife, cutting board

5 Sharpening steel, slicing knife, utility knife, paring knife, wire strainer, rubber scraper, kitchen scale, meat thermometer

123

(This page, from top) Glass and stainless steel double boiler, stainless steel crepe pan, copper teakettle, stainless steel wok with tempura strainer, clay cooker, stainless steel pressure cooker, cast aluminum waffle iron, glass baking dish, ceramic baking dishes.
(Opposite page, from top) Cast aluminum griddle, stainless steel omelet pan, copper au gratin pan, enamel-on-steel saucepan, aluminum stockpot, stainless steel steamer, aluminum fish poaching pan, enameled cast-iron stewpot, cast-iron skillet.

SMALL APPLIANCES

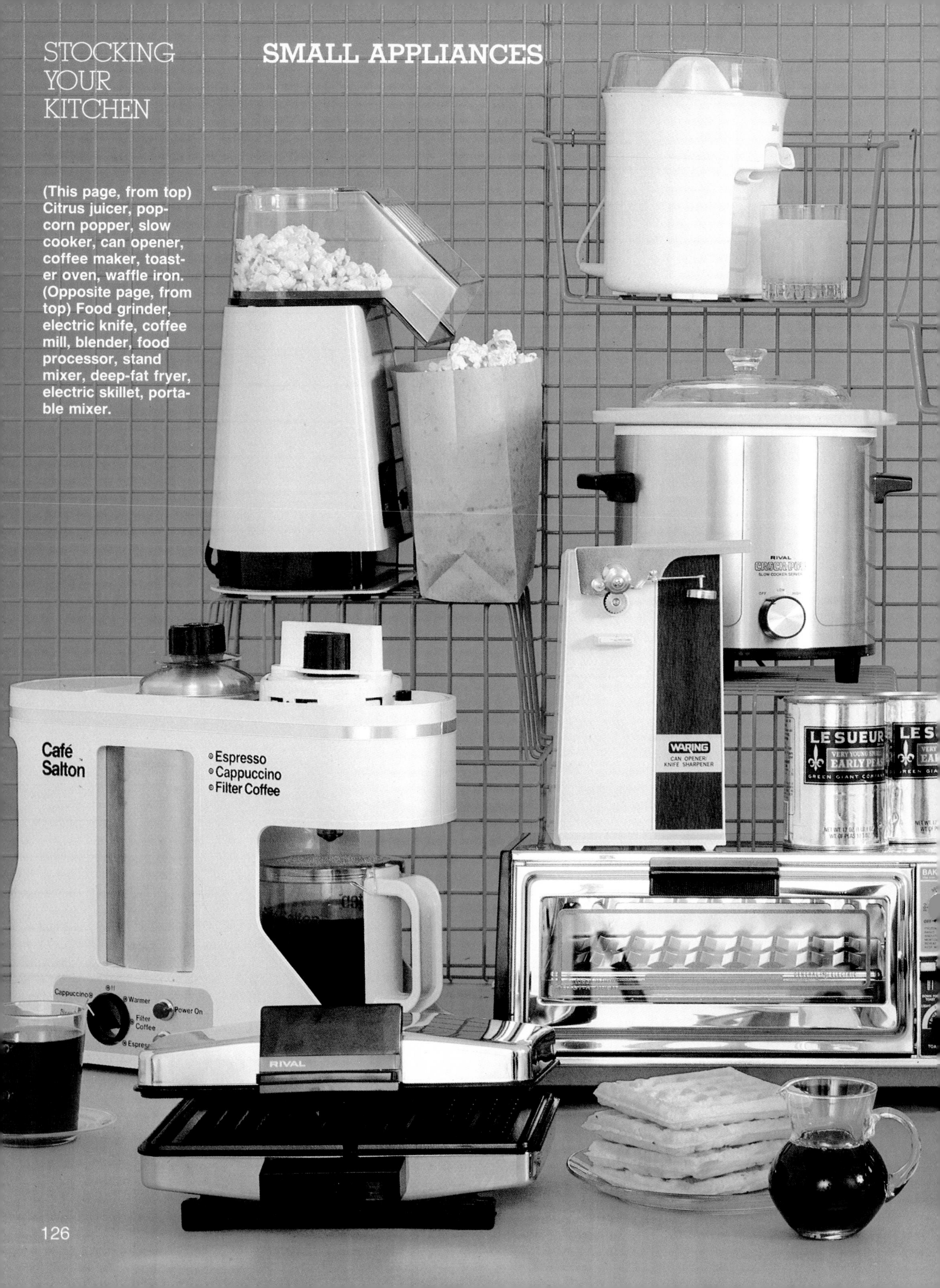

(This page, from top)
Citrus juicer, pop-
corn popper, slow
cooker, can opener,
coffee maker, toast-
er oven, waffle iron.
(Opposite page, from
top) Food grinder,
electric knife, coffee
mill, blender, food
processor, stand
mixer, deep-fat fryer,
electric skillet, porta-
ble mixer.

Café
Salton

○ Espresso
○ Cappuccino
○ Filter Coffee

Cappuccino○   ○ Warmer   ○ Power On
Filter
Coffee
○ Espresso

RIVAL

WARING
CAN OPENER/
KNIFE SHARPENER

RIVAL
CROCK-POT
SLOW COOKER SERIES
OFF   LOW   HIGH

LE SUEUR
VERY YOUNG SMALL
EARLY PEAS
GREEN GIANT COMPANY

LE S.
VERY
EAR

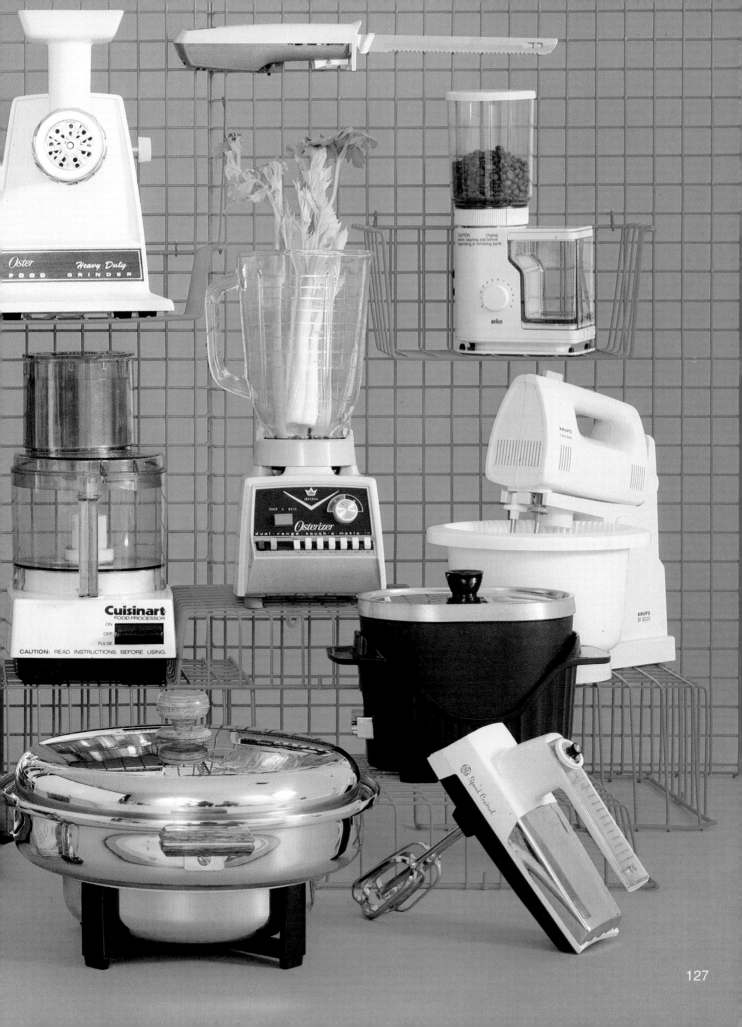

(Opposite page, from top)
Wire whisk, mixing spoon,
grip-handle mixing bowl,
wall scale, nested measuring spoons, mixing bowl,
grater, stacking plastic boxes, funnel, mixing bowls
(ceramic, copper, plastic,

and aluminum), three-way
grater, measuring cups,
freezer paper and tape,
plastic storage bags. (This
page, from top) Aluminum
foil, plastic wrap, screw-top
plastic containers, French
canning jars, kitchen scoop,
plastic pie keeper, mix-and-
serve pitcher, glass liquid
measuring cup, stacking
plastic storage canisters,
see-through storage box
with metal/vinyl lid, sifter,
mix-and-serve jug, see-
through storage boxes.

BASIC GROCERIES

(Top row) Maple syrup, mustard, bouillon cubes, olives, pickles, herbs and spices. (Second row) Rolled oats, hot and cold cereals, tomatoes, tomato sauce, Worcestershire sauce, tomato paste, tuna fish, cream soup, baking powder, vanilla, baking soda, pepper, molasses, unsweetened chocolate, cocoa. (Third row) Raisins, crackers, coffee, honey, soy sauce, minced dried onion, lemon juice, canned soups, chili powder, garlic, gelatin, cornmeal, shortening, browning/seasoning sauce. (Bottom row) Fresh milk, dry milk powder, bread, eggs, cheese, butter, margarine, dried peas, rice, pasta, dried beans, popcorn, peanut butter, vinegar, onions, nuts, chicken broth, catsup, bread crumbs, mayonnaise, olives, oil, sugar, jelly, salt, active dry yeast, brown sugar, all-purpose flour, whole wheat flour, cornstarch.

131

131

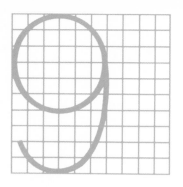

DETAILS

An efficient kitchen is like a tasty dinner—the more attention you pay to details, the more delectable the end result. The twenty ideas presented in this chapter can add spice, variety, style, and—best of all—convenience to any kitchen. You'll see how islands can bring fun and function to a large kitchen, and how storage details can make a small kitchen think it's grown-up. Finally, you'll see how lighting can set just the right mood for work or dining. Details do make a difference.

ISLANDS

A kitchen island serves three important functions. First, it's a work surface that handles both large and small jobs equally well. Next, it adds an extra measure of storage, even in small kitchens. Finally, an island helps direct traffic away from the work center.

The kitchen island shown here does all three jobs with ease. And when soup's on, the two units fold together into a dinette table.

Construction is simple. Use our dimensions or adjust the measurements as necessary.

Cut the ends and backs from a single sheet of ¾-inch birch plywood. The bottoms, dividers, and shelves can be cut from a couple of sheets of ¾-inch fir plywood.

Notch the dividers to accept the ¾x¾-inch rails. Screw and glue together the backs, ends, and bottoms. Attach the dividers, shelves, and rails. Make the framework for the counters from 1x2s, and the counters themselves from ¾-inch fir plywood. Assemble the frames and screw them to the counters, then attach the counter assemblies to the bases. Install a caster at each base corner, top the counters with plastic laminate, and paint the bases. Finally, join them with a piano hinge.

(continued)

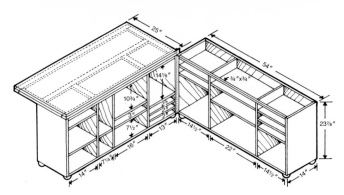

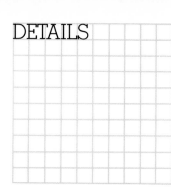

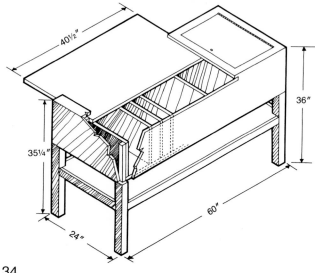

Storing, stirring, serving, or mixing—this peninsula bar does it all. The serving counter slides back to reveal a wealth of storage space. A flip-up lid conceals smaller items. And open shelving below corrals your biggest mixing bowls.

To build the unit, cut 4x4 legs to the lengths shown (one pair is ¾ inch shorter than the other). Cut back the two outside corners of each leg to accept the side and end pieces.

The rest of the unit is built of ¾-inch birch plywood. Begin by cutting the end dividers, which are screwed and glued to the inside faces of the two leg pairs. Next, screw the bottom panel to the bottom of the end dividers.

Attach the outside end panels with screws. The panel on the left side should extend ¾ inch above the tops of the legs. Cut the long side panels so that the portion under the flip-top section is ¾ inch higher than the rest of the panels. Screw the sides to the legs, and then attach the inside divider panels. Add a 1x3 to the top left edge to form a lip over the sliding counter top.

Cut the open shelf panel, notch the corners, and attach to the legs. Trim with 1x2s.

To make the flip-top unit, cut a frame out of plywood so that one edge extends out over the edge of the notches in the side panels, forming the second guide for the sliding top. Cut the door to fit inside the frame, attach it with a piano hinge, then attach the whole unit to the island.

Finish your island bar by cutting a sliding top to fit into its grooves, and giving everything a coat of enamel.

Roll out this island for serving or dining. In the kitchen, it's a sturdy work surface; flip-up end leaves turn it into a 30x72-inch table.

The keys to this rolling island's simple construction are a dozen post connectors, fence-building hardware that will join the wood used to build the basic frame.

The end frames are a pair of 2x4 legs spanned by a 4x4 near the bottom. The tabletop frame is a rectangle of 2x4s; the shelf supports are two 2x4s. Cut all framing pieces first, then paint each piece. Join the pieces with the con-

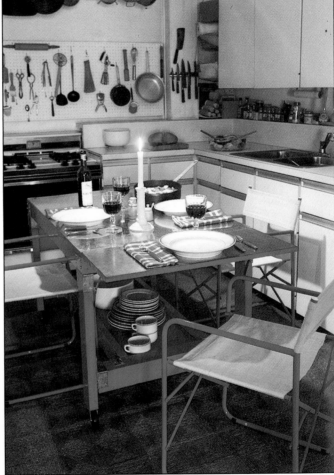

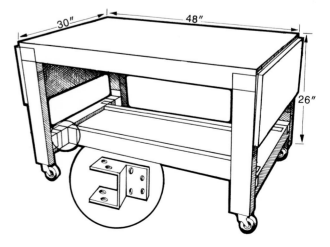

nectors and ¾-inch sheet-metal screws. To complete the shelf support, nail strips of 1x2 lumber around the inside of the shelf frame, leaving a 1½-inch space between the tops of the strips and the tops of the framing members. Do the same for the tabletop, but nail the strips ½ inch from the tops of the frames.

The shelf is simply a piece of ½-inch particleboard cut so that it fits inside its frame and atop the 1x2 strips. You needn't attach the shelf to the frame or the strips.

The tabletop is made from ½-inch particleboard that is cut to fit inside the top frame,

flush with the edges of the frame. Have your materials supplier cut pieces of ¹⁄₁₆-inch galvanized sheet metal to fit the top and the two end leaves. Sand the edges of the metal slightly to dull their sharpness. Glue the metal to the top with contact cement. The end leaves are 1x12s cut to length and topped with sheet metal.

Screw the top to the frame, and attach the leaves with piano hinges so that their surfaces will be flush with the tabletop when raised. Attach two table leg support brackets to each leaf. Finish up with four rubber-wheel casters.

W hy wish for a bigger kitchen when good storage details can produce the same effect? Most kitchens seem cramped only because they waste precious space. The two most common culprits are bulky appliances —blenders and mixers, for instance—and corner base cabinets. Look around your own kitchen and you'll probably find a bit of additional room for most of the problem-solvers shown here.

An extra-deep section of counter—30 inches compared to the usual 25—makes room for the appliance garage shown *below.* You can use standard-depth base cabinets, but you'll have to install them a few inches away from the wall. Insert long screws through the framework at the front of the cabinets to join them to each other. Then screw the cabinets

to the floor to prevent their sliding while you're working at the counter.

If you aren't able to purchase the extra-deep counter, it's fairly simple to make your own. Use 1-inch-thick particleboard or ¾-inch plywood as a base. The laminate covering comes in large sheets that you attach to the base with contact cement. Special edging strips make it simple to finish off the front edge. For best results, follow the recommendations of your laminate dealer.

To keep the appliances out of sight when they're not in use, attach a door to the wall cabinets above. Check your hardware store or home center for glide and hinge ideas. The door pictured here pulls out horizontally, then drops down. Appliances line up along the back wall, leaving clear counter surfaces.

M ost corner cabinets waste almost as much space as they use. It doesn't take long for cookware to work its way into the deep recesses. Check your own corner cabinets and you're likely to find that tube pan you haven't seen for several months.

The best remedy for this problem is to buy a turntable cabinet like the one shown *above.* Although dimensions vary from manufacturer to manufacturer, most units require 12 inches of door space on each side of the corner. Behind the front panels is a three-quarter-round lazy Susan with one or two shelves. If you plan to replace your cabinets anyway, you'll find that a turntable unit costs little or nothing more than buying two 12-inch-wide base cabinets. If you'd rather keep your old cabinets, check with suppliers for a separate turntable mechanism.

And while you're at it, consider installing a turntable unit for wall cabinets. You'll find that small items—spice jars and measuring cups, for instance—are much more accessible when you can bring them front and center.

F ood processors and stand mixers save time and effort, but take up a lot of space. Most are too bulky for permanent countertop status. And when you're using one, you often need a host of bowls, utensils, and foods close by. The flip-up shelf shown *above* solves all these problems in one fell swoop.

To make this idea work well, you'll have to select one base cabinet to serve as the appliance's permanent home. A cabinet that's at least 15 inches wide will ensure that you have sufficient work surface when the shelf is in its raised position.

Check with a hardware supplier to find a set of support arms capable of handling the appliance's weight. The arms screw into the sides of the base cabinet, pivot up, and lock in position. To make the shelf itself, just take a piece of ¾-inch plywood, coat it with contact cement, then cover with plastic laminate. Install an electric outlet inside the cabinet so you'll always be plugged in and ready to go.

A simpler alternative is to install a pullout shelf in a drawer slot. Face a plywood shelf with a drawer front and mount on heavy-duty glides.

Remember when Grandma used to keep her bread in tins on the counter? The close-fitting metal lid kept the moisture content of rolls, pies, and cakes at just the right level.

An updated version of Grandma's tin, *above*, performs the same function. This bread box also serves to keep potatoes and onions high and dry and fresh for months.

To make the box, we removed the bottom from one drawer and then joined it to another to make an extra-deep bin. At a kitchenware store we found a metal bin with a sliding top and set it into the larger bin. The top drawer face was hinged to allow pulling out the slide without interference.

If your drawers are the type with a partition bar between them, you'll have to go to a little more trouble. Remove the partition and the glides that support the upper drawer. Then build a plywood box large enough to fit the space, using the old drawers for guidance. You can reuse your old drawer fronts to provide a facing, or you can fashion a new one from plywood.

Nothing ruins fine cutlery faster than letting it lie loose in a drawer. Blades nick, chip, and dull in almost no time unless you protect them. And if your household has young children, you also want to keep sharp knives away from little fingers.

The slide-out knife rack shown *at right* keeps your knives in tip-top condition, out of harm's way, yet easily reached. To make the unit, use a saber saw to cut a pocket in the end of a cabinet. Attach runners to the inside shelves, and build a side-opening "drawer." To keep the knives in place, attach a strong bar magnet to the back of the rack. Even with the rack in place, you'll have plenty of room left over for small items in the cabinet.

Home farmers and recyclers will appreciate the nifty chopping and waste center *at right*. Dual wastebaskets allow you to sort out compostable kitchen scraps such as vegetable peelings and paper toweling. You also could use one basket for returnable cans and bottles.

The pullout cutting board is mounted on metal drawer glides, and slides out of sight when not in use. A groove in the board catches meat juices for use in gravy. A small metal bowl fits into flanges on the underside of the board to catch drippings that run through a hole in the juice groove.

The wastebasket holder also slides out on drawer glides. A standard base cabinet door hides the baskets after you've emptied their contents.

(continued)

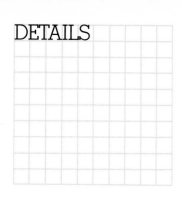

Finding space for pot lids is always a problem. Most of the time, they wind up in a drawer. Getting the one you need usually means taking out all of the lids, then putting back all but the one you want, almost always when you're deeply involved in other cooking tasks.

The special rack shown on the base cabinet door *at right* solves this problem neatly. The rack shown here can be purchased at most hardware or variety stores. Or you can make your own from scraps of wood. To ensure proper clearance, you might have to cut out a section of the cabinet shelf—a small trade-off.

Another nice ready-made is the wrap rack on the upper cabinet door. Access to foil and waxed paper is a snap when the boxes aren't stacked one atop the other. This, too, would make a simple project for anyone handy with wood.

If bringing order to your cabinets leaves you with leftovers, consider what you can do with open storage. The rollaround cart to the left of the cabinets features a pair of wire baskets and a shelf between them. The lower basket is deep enough to store tall bottles. This means you can bring the party to your guests. Glasses go in the top basket; napkins and utensils sit on the shelf.

Above the cart is a colorful wire grid that bolts a few inches away from the wall. Small hooks sewn into the corners of pot holders and hot pads let these items remain within easy reach of the cook.

Let no space go unfilled in your quest for more kitchen storage. That's the philosophy demonstrated in the wire baskets to the right of the base cabinet. What had been an awkward empty niche is now a convenient home for fresh garden produce.

Kitchen cabinets come in standard sizes. Unless you're willing to go to the expense of custom units, you have to make do with 24-inch-deep base cabinets and 12-inch-deep wall cabinets. Standardization makes putting together a kitchen easier, but it also means you might waste a lot of precious space.

Instead of buying custom cabinetry, you can quickly and inexpensively customize standard cabinets. There are literally hundreds of products on the market that can help you bring order and new usable space to your present kitchen cabinets, as all the examples on this page demonstrate.

To these, add the wall unit *at left,* which has plastic tracks attached to its upper surfaces. Clear plastic storage jars slide out along the tracks. Without the usual upper shelf, there's no way to lose sight of items stored on high.

Another nice touch is the mug rack next to the open cabinet door; it's mounted to the wall for quick access.

On the middle shelf in the right-hand cabinet, clear flat plastic containers supplement the hanging jars, offering the same accessibility for somewhat smaller quantities near eye level.

Pantries have gone the way of high button shoes, but the need they served remains. The photograph *at right* shows how you can still incorporate mass storage into a kitchen—without expensive custom cabinetry. The unit along the back corner consists of four standard wall cabinets stacked directly atop a set of base cabinets. The wall units themselves are 36 inches high. Because they are placed lower on the wall than normal, even their top shelves are easily reached all the way to the back.

If you need still more space, look up. In this case, a chain-link fence gate has been hung from screw eyes driven into ceiling joists. Small hooks make it simple to hang pots within reach. Just make certain the gate is securely mounted, preferably over an island so you won't hit your head on the hanging cookware.

The depth of standard base cabinets at floor level can pose a problem when you try to retrieve items stored far in back. The sink cabinet shown at left presents several innovative solutions. A pair of slide-out trays lets you use the full depth of the cabinet to best advantage; you can reach all items without having to become a contortionist. A rack mounted on one door corrals lunch bags (but just as easily could handle dish towels). On the other door hangs a wire mesh basket, which you can line with a plastic bag for trash disposal, or simply use alone for towel storage.

(continued)

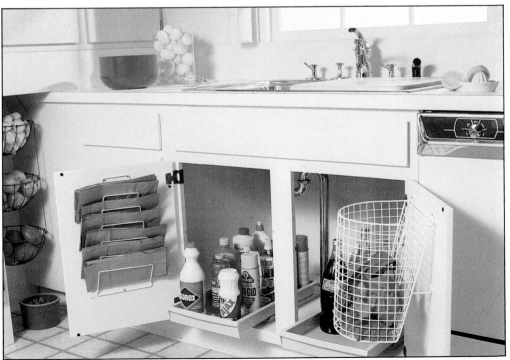

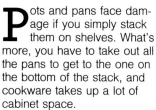

STORAGE
(continued)

Pots and pans face damage if you simply stack them on shelves. What's more, you have to take out all the pans to get to the one on the bottom of the stack, and cookware takes up a lot of cabinet space.

The open storage shown *at right* puts everything out where you can get your hands on it. All you need is a sheet of perforated hardboard and some hooks.

Perforated hardboard—also known as pegboard—is easy to cut with a handsaw or a power saber saw. This means you can shape it to fit even awkward spaces like this stair wall. Mount it on spacers so the hardware used to hang the cookware slips in easily.

For hanging most cookware, look for large hooks. The exposed portion of these can be straight or curved; they come in a variety of sizes. Just be sure you're getting the proper hook for the thickness of the hardboard you've selected; ¼- and ⅛-inch materials require different hooks.

If you want to keep wooden utensils neatly on the wall, look for hardboard tool racks. These pieces of hardware have two sets of rings spaced an inch or so apart. Select a model with rings large enough for you to slip in wooden spoons and other utensils. You also can purchase racks of spring clips that fit into perforated hardboard. These make it easy to suspend utensils that don't have hanging holes.

Storing mugs, cups, and glassware poses a special problem. Unless you stack these items, you use only a fraction of the available space on the shelf—but stacking leads to inevitable chipping and breakage. One good answer is shown *at right*—a drinkware drawer that puts every cubic inch of space to good use and gives excellent protection to fragile pieces.

Of course when you open and close a drawer, cups and glasses tend to slide to and fro, still subject to damage. To eliminate sliding, install dividers in the drawers. This way, each cup or glass gets its own protective niche.

A stainless steel grid system displays pots, pans, and utensils right next to the cook center in the kitchen shown *at right*. Convenience is the main benefit of this type of storage.

To support the gridwork, the owners attached 1x2-inch strips of wood directly to the wall behind the grid. Three strips—at top, center, and bottom—keep the wire away from the wall. Next, 4x8-foot panels of wire grid were cut to fit the space. Wing nuts, threaded onto bolts set into the wood strips, hold the grid in place but allow easy removal when the wall needs cleaning.

A variety of hooks is used to hang utensils from the wirework. For most items, simple S-hooks do the job adequately. L-shaped hooks are used for pots with handles that are out of reach of the S-hooks. A wire rack corrals a number of pot lids. If you can't find hooks to fill a particular need, fashion your own from heavy wire.

To make the dividers, go to your lumberyard and ask for "parting stop," a wood lath that comes in ½x¾-inch strips. Cut the strips to the dimensions of your drawer. Next cut notches in the strips so they can fit together into a grid; the distance between the notches depends on the size of the cups, mugs, or glasses you'll be storing. Each notch should be about ⅜ inch deep and ½ inch across. The wider ¾-inch faces of the parting stop should then form the sides of the partitions. After you've constructed the grid assembly, simply set it into the drawer. You can easily remove it for cleaning.

Good lighting is one detail you shouldn't take for granted in your kitchen. When planning kitchen lighting, remember that you have three types of illumination to consider, and that each serves a different purpose.

• *General lighting* is designed to brighten a whole room. Overhead fixtures that flood large areas with light are the most frequently used for this purpose.

• *Task lighting* provides an extra measure of brightness at specific work stations. Task lighting is offered by fixtures placed close to the work surface, so you don't end up working in your own shadow.

• *Mood lighting* highlights some areas and lets others recede into the shadows. Though the most dramatic, this type of lighting is often the most difficult to achieve; we've gathered a few ideas to help jog your creativity. The three settings shown here demonstrate uses for general, task, and mood lighting that you can adapt to your kitchen. To learn more about kitchen lighting, see pages 94 and 95.

Set a festive mood for dining with an illuminated roll-about cart, shown *above*. Basically, the unit is an electrified tea cart. You can purchase the cart itself or build it. The excitement begins when you install a pair of fluorescent fixtures underneath the top shelf. The two bulbs provide just enough light to bounce off the middle shelf and illuminate the area around the cart.

Run the bulbs' wiring to a duplex outlet box mounted on the cart. A power cord and plug run from the box to a nearby wall outlet. Plug an electric wok or skillet into the cart's outlet box and you're ready for tableside cookery.

A similar scheme also works for more stationary furnishings. The combination buffet table and planter shown *at left* is simple to build. The skirting around the top shelf conceals a pair of 48-inch fluorescent tubes. The rosy glow comes from a pair of plant lights installed in the fixture.

The box holding the potted plants has a bottom tray for drips and spills. You also can line the box's sides and bottom with plastic.

For a large plant collection, just add more shelves and fluorescent fixtures.

General lighting should be indirect—aimed to bounce off pale walls or ceiling and then into the room. Bouncing diffuses the light for even illumination over the entire area.

Task lighting should go directly from fixture to work surface, providing brighter light for close work. It is vital that the task light comes from over the counter to eliminate shadows.

The peninsula work center on this page provides both general and task lighting. Its secret hides in the boxed area under the glassware shelf.

A pair of fluorescent tubes inside are covered at top and bottom with frosted diffusion panels. For general lighting, the light bounces off the ceiling and the underside of the top shelf. These same bulbs also provide task lighting for the work surface beneath.

To get task lighting on regular counters, mount fluorescent fixtures under wall cabinets. Lacking wall cabinets over a counter, use hanging fixtures or recessed spotlights directly above.

For general lighting, figure on about 90 watts of fluorescent lighting per 120 square feet of kitchen; to illuminate the same area with incandescent lighting, figure on about 250 watts. Incandescent bulbs are your best choice for lighting a planning desk where you will be doing a lot of reading.

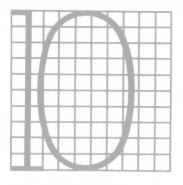

KITCHEN KEEPING

Most of this book has been devoted to ways you can make your kitchen more attractive and convenient. Now for a few pages about keeping it that way. Here's how to get through cleanup jobs quickly and efficiently; how to diagnose, repair, and prevent component malfunctions; and how to assure that the busiest room in your house is also one of the safest. And if there's a disabled person in your household, he or she especially will appreciate learning about ways to adapt kitchen work centers to the needs of a wheelchair-user.

CLEANING KITCHEN SURFACES

	REGULAR CARE
WALLS AND CABINETS	
Paint/wall coverings	Wash in small sections; use detergent solution.
Prefinished wood surfaces	Dust; use wax or oil-base polish; wipe with grain.
FLOORS	
Resilient	Dust-mop, sweep, or vacuum; damp-mop.
Wood	Dry-mop; damp-mop; avoid too much water.
Carpeting	Vacuum daily.
Tile/slate	Dust-mop; vacuum; damp-mop.
COUNTERS	
Plastic	Wipe with damp sponge, mild detergent solution.
Wood	Damp-sponge; dry. Avoid too much water.
Hard-surface	Wipe with sudsy water; dry with soft cloth.
APPLIANCES, SINKS, AND COOKWARE	
Baked-on enamel	Rinse with soap and water.
Porcelain	Scrub daily with detergent and hot water.
Stainless steel	Wash with hot suds; rinse; dry.
Aluminum	Rinse with hot water; polish with soft cloth.
Glass	Use hot water and detergent on glassware, special cleaner on windows.

SPOT/STAIN REMOVAL	SPECIAL TREATMENTS
Use degreaser on oily spots and stains.	Use wallpaper cleaner on non-washable wall coverings.
Use appliance cleaner-wax on sticky, oily spots.	Avoid using too much water on wood; use appliance cleaner-wax on oily polish accumulation.
Scrub with mild detergent: apply appliance wax; scrape carefully with a sharp knife.	Use polish with sealer on older porous types; liquid wax on waxables; special dressing on no-wax types.
Sanding, refinishing may be necessary.	Use solvent-base polish to clean and wax; buff with electric polisher or by hand.
Use aerosol cleaner or absorbent powder.	Have professionally cleaned; avoid excess water, dry quickly; check colorfastness before cleaning.
For grease, use household cleanser or washing soda.	Add protective vegetable-oil-base sealer to quarry tile that will be subjected to grease.
Apply chlorine bleach solution; don't use abrasives.	Apply protective finish such as automotive cleaner-wax or appliance wax.
Use 50% ammonia solution; fine steel wool on scratches.	Keep wood from drying out; brush on a warm coat of mineral oil every month, let stand overnight.
On oily spots use degreaser; water spots, special cleaner.	Use creamy liquid wax on tile, furniture cream or kitchen polish on stainless steel.
Use chlorine bleach on stains.	Spray with non-stick finish after each cleaning for easier care.
Use mild scouring powder or chlorine bleach solution.	Mix a paste of cream of tartar and hydrogen peroxide for scrubbing especially persistent stains.
Use fine steel wool and fine scouring powder.	Heat stains cannot be removed. Use good silver polish to restore dulled finishes.
Use steel wool pads, rubbing in one direction only.	Use commercial aluminum cleaner on freshly washed, still-warm metal; dry with soft cloth.
Remove stains or cloudiness with ammonia/water solution.	Use commercial cleaner; or mix cool water with vinegar, washing soda, kerosene, or alcohol; dry with lint-free cloths or paper, or use a squeegee.

INSECTS AND ODORS

Keeping your kitchen clean, dry, and well-ventilated prevents odor and insect problems better than any magic spray.

If you have odor troubles, find the source and eliminate it.

• Empty kitchen waste containers daily. Wash them with disinfectant and dry before putting in a new liner.

• Flush disposers with water once a week. Remove odor-causing matter by grinding ice cubes or small bones.

• Cover all foods in the refrigerator. Add an open box of baking soda to absorb odors.

If pests invade, find their point of entry first. Check for small cracks or crevices in the house foundation or around windows and doors. Vacuum, dust, and clean all surfaces with a disinfectant. Vacuum up spider webs and egg sacs and discard the cleaner bag at once. Apply a safe insecticide to all surfaces and let dry.

When using sprays in food preparation areas, cover all food, cooking utensils, and dishes. If any items have been exposed, wash in hot water and detergent before using. Discard exposed food. Store all insecticides away from heat and light and out of children's reach.

REPAIRING AND MAINTAINING KITCHEN COMPONENTS

TROUBLESHOOTING KITCHEN MALFUNCTIONS

	SYMPTOM	CAUSE
PLUMBING		
Drains	Sink stopped up; sink drains slowly; disposer stopped up.	Grease, garbage, coffee grounds, or other matter blocking the pipes.
Faucets	Dripping from the spout; other leaks.	Washer worn; faucet seat packing worn; O-ring or spout O-ring burred.
Pipes	Water pipes leaking.	Pipe worn or connection inadequate.
	Water hammer.	Air chambers filled with water.
Food waste disposer	Disposer will not run.	Power not reaching unit; matter is wedged against a cutting edge.
Porcelain	Finish on sink chipped.	Severe blow to surface.
APPLIANCES		
Electric range	Surface element doesn't heat.	Element or terminal block defective.
	Oven fails to maintain set temperature.	Thermostat not properly calibrated.
Gas range	Surface burner not lighting.	Ports in pilot or burner clogged.
	Oven won't light.	Pilot out; automatic timer is not set properly.
Refrigerator	Refrigerator runs but doesn't cool.	Controls defective; controls improperly set; air ducts blocked.
Dishwasher	Will not fill, or overfills.	Float switch defective.
	Dishes not cleaning.	Spray arm clogged; spray arm not rotating properly; water temperature not high enough.
CABINETS, WALLS, AND FLOORS		
Latches	Cabinet door won't stay shut.	Catch defective.
Hinges	Cabinet door sticks shut.	Hinge loose; door catch out of position; door and frame not fitting properly.
Drawers	Drawer sticking.	Runners rough; dampness; joints or runners loose.
Surfaces	Dark burn marks or charred areas on wood.	High heat in direct contact with wood.
	Scorch or burn mark on resilient flooring.	High heat in direct contact with flooring.

SOLUTION

Use a plunger or auger snake; clean the trap; use cleaner only in slow drains, never in one that's completely clogged.

Replace washer; if drips persist, dress or replace faucet seat. Repack; replace ring; replace entire faucet.

Wrap pipe with plastic electrician's tape or use clamps with rubber surround to stop leak; replace pipe.

Drain entire plumbing system with faucets open to admit fresh air to chambers; close faucets and refill.

Check overload switch, fuse, or circuit breaker on unit; using a broomstick, move cutter backward to free wedged matter.

Clean chipped area; retouch with porcelain epoxy.

Remove element and try in another terminal block; replace element; replace terminal block.

Recalibrate or replace thermostat.

Relight pilot; clean out ports with a pin or paper clip.

Relight pilot; switch timer to manual setting.

Adjust controls; replace controls; remove air obstructions around all sides; dust rear coils.

Lift float to check for free movement; replace if defective.

Clean holes in spray arm; check for obstructions in spray arm path; increase household water heater temperature.

Tighten latch adjustment screw; install a magnetic catch.

Tighten screws; adjust catch; shim the hinge so door fits the frame; plane areas that stick.

Wax or soap runners and drawer edges; plane areas that stick; reglue joints or runners in place.

Use commercial cleaner or rottenstone and oil paste on surface burns; scrape away charred areas and spot-refinish deep burns with artists' oil paints.

Cut a square out of old flooring and piece in a new one; apply with adhesive; weight for 24 hours before using.

OUNCES OF PREVENTION

Keep your kitchen equipment in top-notch shape and you'll be rewarded with years of nonstop service.

Refrigerator
Every three months or so, move your refrigerator out to the middle of the room and vacuum or dust the condenser coils underneath. If you have an automatic-defrost model, remove the water-evaporating tray at the bottom of the refrigerator and wash and dry it well before replacing; defrost a manual-defrost refrigerator when the frost becomes about ¼ inch thick.

Kitchen range
Remove and clean the screen or filter on your range's ventilating hood often—once a week if you use it daily. At least twice a year, wash the grease off the fan and clean inside the ductwork as far as you can reach; for the rest, get a professional as needed. Built-up grease creates a fire hazard.

Waste disposer
Use your food waste disposer as the manufacturer recommends. It's not supposed to be able to devour everything; don't put corn husks, artichokes, seafood shells, wood, glass, paper, metal, or plastic in it. On the other hand, hard materials such as small bones or ice cubes remove grease as they knock against the sides of the grinding chamber. Run the unit until all particles have passed through the disposer. Apply these maintenance remedies every few weeks to prevent clogged drains.

General maintenance
Appliances don't just look better when they are clean—they work better, too. Dust, grease, and food particles literally gum up the works, so it makes good sense to wipe up spills and drips as they happen. And it only takes a minute to clean work surfaces after each meal.

Keep manufacturers' instructions for all appliances where you can refer to them easily. They offer tips for prolonging the life of your kitchen helpmates.

Also keep lubricants in the kitchen and use them often. Oil, petroleum jelly, and graphite will keep many appliances operating like new. Lubricate as recommended by manufacturers—before problems start.

Don't overwork your kitchen appliances. They are meant for normal household use. If you need to run one for an extended period of time, give it a chance to cool off every so often. Overheating will burn out motors and other essential parts.

DEALING WITH
KITCHEN MISHAPS

Safety first should be embroidered on a sampler for prominent display in every kitchen. A gust of wind blows a curtain into an open burner flame. Teetering on a chair, you stretch for a top shelf, slip, and fall. Someone receives a potentially deadly shock from an ungrounded appliance. You probably already know most of the commonsense measures that can make a kitchen safe, but here's a refresher course.

HOW SAFE IS YOUR KITCHEN?

To find out if your kitchen harbors an accident in the making, give yourself this quiz. A single *yes* answer means you'd better take corrective action.

Fire hazards
☐ Do appliance plugs feel hot to the touch? (If so, a circuit is overloaded.)
☐ Are receptacles the old-fashioned, two-slot, non-grounded type? (Today's building codes call for grounding-type receptacles.)
☐ Do you cheat a few extra amps out of a circuit by using a bigger fuse than the wiring was designed to handle?
☐ Are flexible gas connection lines out in the open where they can be kicked or bent?
☐ Do you use flimsy extension cords on appliances? (They should be heavy-duty types no more than a foot or so longer than you need.)
☐ Do you use flammable substances such as aerosols in cooking or baking areas?
☐ Do you let grease build up in hoods, vents, and flues?
☐ Do you keep cloth and paper near the range?
☐ Have you put off buying a fire extinguisher?
☐ Are you unsure about how to shut off your home's main electrical circuit?
☐ Do some appliances have worn plugs or frayed cords?

Shock hazards
Most of the electrical items we've identified as fire hazards also can give you a dangerous shock. In addition, take care always to keep water and electricity away from each other. And never interpose yourself between the two—current could move through your body on its way to ground. Here are some specifically shock-related questions; again, one *yes* could spell trouble.
☐ Do you sometimes clean or service small appliances while they're plugged in?
☐ Do you keep a radio, clock, or other electrical item near the sink, where it could fall in?
☐ When bread gets stuck in a toaster, do you reach for a metal utensil to dislodge it?

Asphyxiation hazards
Natural and LP gas come scented with a distinctive odor that you can smell when there's a leak; carbon monoxide, a by-product of combustion, is odorless and just as lethal. If you smell gas, open windows and call your power company.

Carbon monoxide isn't likely to be a problem in most kitchens unless there's a furnace, water heater, or garage access nearby. If you or someone else, especially children or pets, feels unaccountably faint, get outside for fresh air; if the faintness disappears, suspect carbon monoxide. Here are some other gas-related points to consider.

☐ Are your gas appliances without individual shutoff valves?
☐ Are you unsure where your home's main gas shutoff is located and how to operate it? (Some have a handle you can turn manually; others, a bar-type key that must be moved with a wrench. When the handle or bar is parallel to the pipe, gas is flowing through; when it's perpendicular to the pipe, gas is shut off.)
☐ If gas service is interrupted, have you inadvertently left a burner on?

Other kitchen hazards
☐ Do you use a chair or wobbly step stool to reach high places?
☐ Do you let slippery spills lie until you get around to cleaning them up?
☐ Does traffic channel through rather than around work areas?
☐ Are cabinet drawers left open when they're not in use?
☐ Do appliance doors block traffic when they're open?
☐ Are some areas of your kitchen dimly lit?
☐ Do you just toss knives into a drawer, rather than provide them with safe storage?
☐ Do you keep trash in a loose bag or sack?
☐ Do you let pot handles project from the side or front of the range?
☐ Do your scatter rugs have slippery backings?

WHAT TO DO IF FIRE BREAKS OUT

Kitchens run a close second as the most likely area of the house to have a fire. (Living rooms are first, believe it or not.) With exposed heating surfaces and open flames, it's no wonder that fire can break out in a kitchen almost any time.

Once a fire starts
Don't stop thinking; keep your wits about you. Clear thinking and positive action will snuff out most fires before they have a chance to spread.

If a small pan on top of the range begins to blaze, turn off the heat immediately and smother the flames with a tight-fitting lid or a cookie sheet. Or, use a fire extinguisher of the dry chemical or carbon dioxide type (more about extinguishers later). If you haven't been able to stop the fire, leave the house and call the fire department from the closest phone you can find *away* from your house. Don't risk carrying a flaming pan out of the house.

If your clothing ignites
Drop to the floor and roll in a rug, blanket, or coat to smother the flames. *Do not run!* As a safety precaution, don't wear garments with loose sleeves when you cook or are near cooking surfaces. And keep pan han-

dles away from the edge of the range.

A fire in the broiler
Turn the heat off and close the door. After a few minutes, open the door a crack to see if the flames have died down. If they haven't, use a dry chemical or carbon dioxide fire extinguisher and close the door until the fire is completely out.

If you smell gas
First, open a nearby window to ventilate the kitchen. Then call your utility company or an appliance service firm for an immediate inspection. (Check to see whether range burners are off and the pilot light is lit.)

Extinguishing fires
A mixture of baking soda and salt often will smother the flames of a pan fire. Above all, *don't use water*. You might choose to keep boxes of soda and salt close to your range. Better yet, keep on hand a fire extinguisher suited to the types of fire you might encounter in your kitchen.

Fire extinguishers are rated by the letters A, B, and C. Class A fires are of normal combustibles such as wood, paper, and the like; water works fine with these,

so you really don't need a Class A extinguisher. Class B includes flammable and combustible liquids; Class C involves live electrical equipment. Since most kitchen fires start as Class B or C fires, an extinguisher for Class B:C is ideal for this work area.

You'll want to locate it in the path of exit from the kitchen so you can grab the extinguisher on the way out, move back in when you're ready to attack the flames, and escape if the fire gets out of hand. Always leave yourself an escape route.

Involve the whole family
Have all family members read and understand the operating instructions for your fire extinguishers. Many families also conduct home fire drills. Each member of the family should know what to do in case of a fire and how to exit safely—not just from the kitchen, but from all areas of the house.

Involve the entire family in fire prevention, too. Stress safety to young children as soon as they're old enough to understand. With older children, review the basics listed here and on the opposite page.

And by all means, invest a few dollars in two or three smoke detectors. With better units, you can adjust the sensitivity so the alarm won't go off every time you broil a steak or burn a piece of French toast.

CHILD-PROOFING YOUR KITCHEN

Kitchens pose a special hazard for inquisitive little fingers. If you have children under the age of six, a few special precautions could spare you a high-speed trip to the hospital.

Start by considering what your kitchen looks like from a small child's point of view. Are cleaners, bleaches, waxes, cleaning fluids, and pesticides accessible? Simply stashing them on a high shelf may not be adequate safety; instead fit one cabinet with a safety latch or lock and keep dangerous substances in there.

Some households also paint the lids of harmful materials bright red, or even stencil them with a skull and crossbones; younger children can learn to avoid these by the color or symbol.

Don't mix harmful things in any container that is also used for food preparation, or that might be mistaken for anything else. Shop for goods with child-proof lids, and always replace the tops after use.

What about range controls? If they're near the front of the unit within children's reach, consider investing in a new stove—at the very least, remove the handles except when you're preparing meals.

OUTFITTING FOR A DISABLED PERSON

FORWARD REACH OVER OBSTACLE

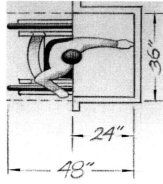

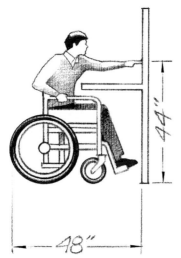

HIGH FORWARD REACH

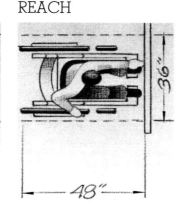

SINK CLEARANCE

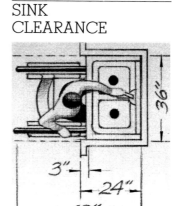

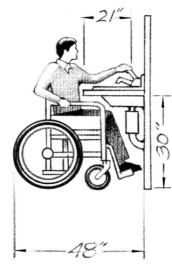

COOKTOP CLEARANCE

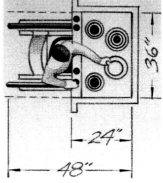

The first step in planning a kitchen for a disabled person is to determine how that person wants to use the area. At one end of the kitchen remodeling scale, a few simple alterations make the kitchen function well for anyone; at the other end is a totally wheelchair-designed kitchen—remodeled from the floor up especially to suit the needs of a disabled person.

First study the *work triangle*—the sink-to-range-to-refrigerator traffic path discussed in Chapter 4. To accommodate a wheelchair, the path connect-

ing the three major work areas must allow for maneuvering without enlarging the triangle. To make it bigger would mean a lot of extra cross-kitchen traveling just to accomplish a simple task.

Basic alterations for the wheelchair cook
Accessibility to appliances and storage is vital. Here's where the design standards shown above come in.
• The work counter top should be no less than 24 inches deep and no more than 30 inches from the floor.

• A free space 36 inches wide and at least 27 inches high under the work area will enable a wheelchair-user to pull his or her knees under the counter top. To accommodate the armrests of the wheelchair under the counter top as well, the free space under the work area should measure 36 inches wide, 30 inches high, and 24 inches deep. This extends one's forward reach to 24 inches—the full depth of standard kitchen counter tops.
• The sink should sit no higher than 34 inches from the floor, and have a single-lever fitting

no farther than 21 inches from the front edge of the counter. The sink itself should be no more than 5 inches deep and recessed about 3 inches from the front of the counter to provide free space for elbow support. Reserve knee space under the sink, too.

You may be able to modify existing cabinets to make the desirable knee space under the work surface and sink by removing the doors, central rail, and toe board, and cutting back the cabinet floor. To bring the counter top to a wheelchair cook, install pullout

Planning a barrier-free kitchen for a disabled person challenges your design ingenuity. The remodeled room has to meet the special needs of a wheelchair-user —our focus here—and still be convenient, safe, and comfortable for everyone else in the house. Here are the specific design criteria you need to know.

lap boards located around the kitchen. Place them about 30 inches from the floor, which will allow their use from either the front or the sides.

Indeed, if you're planning to make the kitchen as convenient as possible, you may decide to provide work areas all around the room that are only 30 inches high.

Adapting appliances
When choosing your appliances, give special consideration to safety features. The best cooking appliance for persons in wheelchairs is not a freestanding range. Instead, it's a cooktop like the one shown in the drawing *opposite, far right*. Its controls are mounted at the front and the heating elements are staggered so the cook never has to reach across a front unit to put a pot on one at the rear. Choose wall-mounted ovens and microwave units that open from the side rather than the top, which will permit their positioning at a height convenient to a disabled person.

Install a refrigerator with slide-out drawers and also a low-mounted slide-out freezer.

Check the doors; their width could be a barrier to a wheelchair-user.

Small electric appliances are great helpmates for a disabled cook. Just make sure that your kitchen's electrical circuits can handle the load. If necessary, place additional outlets so they'll be within the wheelchair cook's reach.

Realigning storage
Standard kitchen storage arrangements—floor- or wall-mounted—won't work for most wheelchair-users since, for the most part, they are mounted out of a seated person's reach. Drawers, lazy Susans, and pegboards all help to alleviate this problem. Consider replacing standard cabinets with units that have easily reachable drawers or turntables instead of the usual stationary shelves. A barrier-free kitchen like the one shown *above* is a wheelchair cook's dream. It eliminates everyday obstacles and modifies existing spaces to suit a disabled person's needs.

WHERE TO GO FOR MORE INFORMATION

Better Homes and Gardens® Books

Would you like to learn more about decorating, remodeling, or maintaining your kitchen? These Better Homes and Gardens® books can help.

Better Homes and Gardens®
NEW DECORATING BOOK
How to translate ideas into workable solutions for every room in your home. Choosing a style, furniture arrangements, windows, walls and ceilings, floors, lighting, and accessories. 433 color photos, 76 how-to illustrations, 432 pages.

Better Homes and Gardens®
COMPLETE GUIDE TO HOME REPAIR,
MAINTENANCE, & IMPROVEMENT
Inside your home, outside your home, your home's systems, basics you should know. Anatomy and step-by-step drawings illustrate components, tools, techniques, and finishes. 515 how-to techniques, 75 charts, 2,734 illustrations, 552 pages.

Better Homes and Gardens®
COMPLETE GUIDE TO GARDENING
A comprehensive guide for beginners and experienced gardeners. Houseplants, lawns and landscaping, trees and shrubs, greenhouses, insects and diseases. 461 color photos, 434 how-to illustrations, 37 charts, 552 pages.

Better Homes and Gardens®
STEP-BY-STEP
BASIC PLUMBING
Getting to know your system, solving plumbing problems, making plumbing improvements, plumbing basics and procedures. 42 projects, 200 illustrations, 96 pages.

Better Homes and Gardens®
STEP-BY-STEP
BASIC WIRING
Getting to know your system, solving electrical problems, making electrical improvements, electrical basics and procedures. 22 projects, 286 illustrations, 96 pages.

Better Homes and Gardens®
STEP-BY-STEP
BASIC CARPENTRY
Setting up shop, choosing tools and building materials, mastering construction techniques, building boxes, hanging shelves, framing walls, installing drywall and paneling. 10 projects, 191 illustrations, 96 pages.

Better Homes and Gardens®
STEP-BY-STEP
MASONRY & CONCRETE
Choosing tools and materials, planning masonry projects, working with concrete, working with brick, block, and stone, special-effect projects. 10 projects, 200 drawings, 96 pages.

Better Homes and Gardens®
STEP-BY-STEP
HOUSEHOLD REPAIRS
Basic tools for repair jobs, repairing walls and ceilings, floors and stairs, windows and doors, and electrical and plumbing items. 200 illustrations, 96 pages.

Better Homes and Gardens®
STEP-BY-STEP
CABINETS AND SHELVES
Materials and hardware, planning guidelines, the ABCs of cabinet construction, cutting and joining techniques, project potpourri. 155 illustrations, 96 pages.

Other Sources of Information

Most professional associations publish lists of their members, and will be happy to furnish these lists upon request. They also may offer educational material and other information.

American Gas Association (AGA)
1515 Wilson Blvd.
Arlington, VA 22209
Membership includes distribution and transmission companies, local utilities, and pipelines. The association promotes energy conservation and does testing of gas appliances for safety and efficiency.

American Home Lighting Institute
230 N. Michigan Ave.
Chicago, IL 60601
Membership includes manufacturers, distributors, and retailers of residential lighting fixtures. The institute also trains lighting specialists.

National Kitchen and Bath Association (NKBA)
114 Main Street
Hackettstown, NJ 07840
Members have agreed to abide by and practice the bylaws and codes of ethics for the kitchen/bathroom industry. NKBA also publishes an annual directory of certified kitchen designers and another of accredited kitchen specialists, called Certified Kitchen Dealers (CKD).

ACKNOWLEDGMENTS

Association of Home Appliance Manufacturers (AHAM)
20 N. Wacker Dr.
Chicago, IL 60606
Membership includes the largest manufacturers of major and small appliances. It administers four voluntary appliance-certification programs that show the capacity ratings of all models of room air conditioners, refrigerators, freezers, humidifiers, and dehumidifiers. This information is designed to help consumers select the right capacity appliance for their needs, and is published in a directory twice a year (information on room air conditioners is published quarterly).

Major Appliance Consumer Action Panel (MACAP)
20 N. Wacker Dr.
Chicago, IL 60606
This panel receives correspondence and complaints from appliance owners, studies industry practices, and advises industry of ways to improve service. It also reports to consumers about best appliance performance. Individual complaints are forwarded to an executive of the manufacturer of the product involved.

National Association of the Remodeling Industry (NARI)
11 E. 44th St.
New York, NY 10017
Membership includes contractors, manufacturers, wholesalers, lenders, utilities, and publishers. The association promotes the common business interests of the remodeling industry.

National Housewares Manufacturers Association (NHMA)
1130 Merchandise Mart
Chicago, IL 60654
Membership includes manufacturers of housewares and small appliances. A semiannual trade show takes place in Chicago.

Tile Council of America
Box 326
Princeton, NJ 08540
Membership includes manufacturers of ceramic tile. Booklets are available on how to best use ceramic tile, as well as information about do-it-yourself installation.

Architects and Designers

Following is a page-by-page listing of the architects and designers whose work appears in this book.

Pages 8-9
  Ken Kurtzman, Steinqu, Kurtzman
Page 10
  Karin Weller
Page 11
  Carol Barnes
Pages 12-13
  James Caldwell
Pages 14-15
  Nan Rosenblatt
Pages 16-17
  Luiz Salazar
Pages 18-19
  St. Charles Kitchens
Pages 26-27
  Peri Wolfman
  Sheila Hobgood
Pages 30-31
  Joel D'Orazio
Pages 32-33
  Eugene Futterman
Pages 36-37
  Ted Haggett; Adelaide Osborne/Cybele Interiors
Pages 40-41
  Merle Kleweno and William Sarbacker
Pages 42-43
  Irena Martens
Pages 44-45
  Ted Kloss
Pages 48-49
  Richard Buford; Ward Seymour
Pages 52-53
  House of Denmark; Jack Sidener; RuthL Kitchens
Pages 56-57
  The Design Concern
Pages 66-67
  Bill Johnson
Pages 68-69
  Stephen Mead
Pages 70-71
  Robert H. Stoecker; Ted Tessler; Robert Herman Associates

Pages 72-73
  William Ketcham General Electric Co.
Pages 74-75
  Charles Liddy
Pages 76-77
  David Ashe
Pages 98-99
  Ryland Koets, Architects and Associates
Pages 100-101
  Fred Hulten, contractor
Pages 102-103
  Peter J. Pfister
Pages 110-111
  Marta MacDonald
Pages 112-113
  John Este-Perkins; Jeannine Bazer
Page 115
  Barry Berkus
Pages 116-117
  Carl Safe; Linda Joan Smith
Pages 118-119
  James V. Pruitt & Kirk Heiser for Lord & Burnham
Pages 132-133
  Louisa Cowan, Armstrong Design
Pages 136-137
  The Design Concern
Pages 138-139
  The Design Concern
Pages 140-141
  Ted Tessler; Wallace French
Pages 142-143
  The Design Concern

Photographers and Illustrators

We extend our thanks to the following photographers and illustrators whose creative talents and technical skills contributed much to this book.

Ernest Braun, Jim Buckels, Ross Chapple, Peter M. Fine, John Gregory, Harry Hartman, Hedrich-Blessing, Hellman Design Associates, Inc., Bill Helms, William N. Hopkins, Bill Hopkins, Jr., Fred Lyon, Marine Arts, Maris/Semel, Bradley Olman.

TEMPLATES
TO HELP YOU
PLAN

APPLIANCES

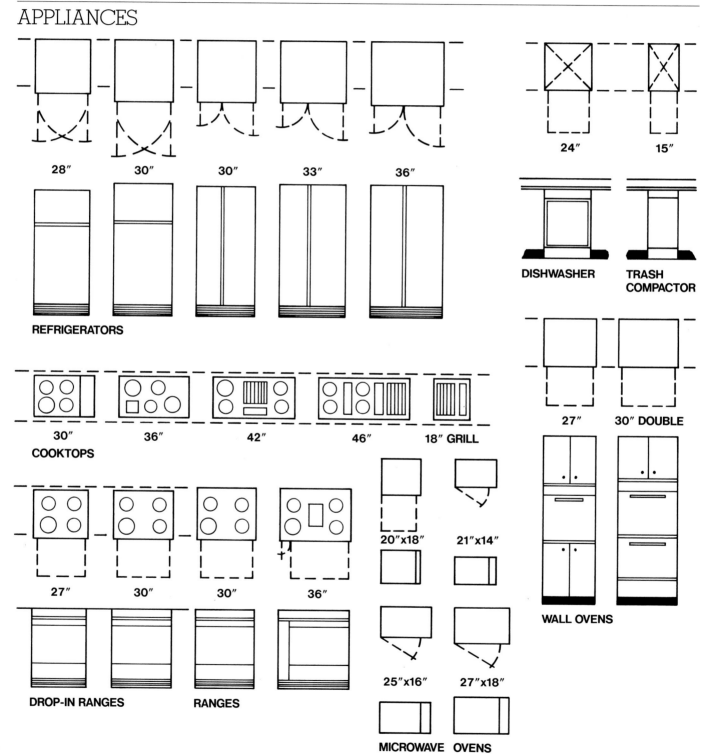

28″   30″   30″   33″   36″

REFRIGERATORS

24″   15″

DISHWASHER   TRASH
               COMPACTOR

30″   36″   42″   46″   18″ GRILL

COOKTOPS

27″   30″ DOUBLE

27″   30″   30″   36″

20″x18″   21″x14″

DROP-IN RANGES   RANGES

WALL OVENS

25″x16″   27″x18″

MICROWAVE OVENS

SINK BASES

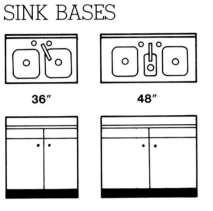

36"   **48"**

Most of the draw-
ings on these
pages show both
an overhead view
and an elevation
view. The overhead
views are what you
will be tracing for
your floor plans; the
elevations are pro-
vided to help you
visualize the units.
In several cases
(sinks, for example)
in which the actual
appliance or cabi-
net could be of vari-
ous styles, we've
shown a basic
model—the primary
concern being the
amount of space
it occupies in the
floor plan. To learn
more about using
these templates,
see pages 62-79.

30"

WALL CABINETS

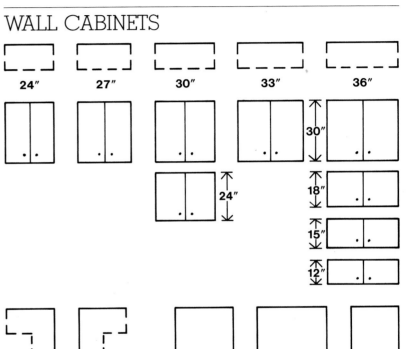

24"   **27"**   **30"**   **33"**   **36"**

30"

24"

18"

15"

12"

RIGHT CORNER   **LEFT CORNER**

30" PANTRY   **36" PANTRY**   **24" BROOM**

ANGLE CORNER

(continued)

TEMPLATES TO HELP YOU PLAN
(continued)

BASE CABINETS

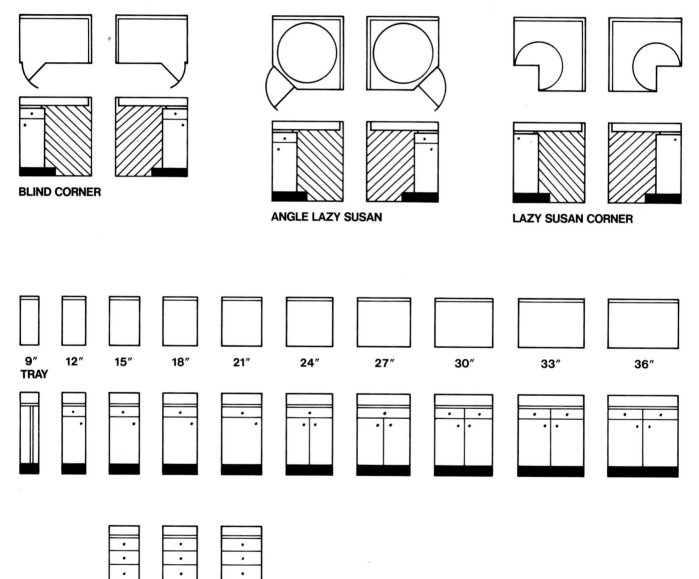

BLIND CORNER

ANGLE LAZY SUSAN

LAZY SUSAN CORNER

| 9″ TRAY | 12″ | 15″ | 18″ | 21″ | 24″ | 27″ | 30″ | 33″ | 36″ |

INDEX

INDEX
(continued)

Have BETTER HOMES AND
GARDENS® magazine delivered to your door. For information, write to: MR. ROBERT
AUSTIN, P.O. BOX 4536, DES
MOINES, IA 50336.